The Best Dressed List

Classroom Trends and Cultural Fashions

Susan J. Huber

A SCARECROWEDUCATION BOOK

The Scarecrow Press, Inc.
Lanham, Maryland, and Oxford
2003

A SCARECROWEDUCATION BOOK

Published in the United States of America
by Scarecrow Press, Inc.
A Member of the Rowman & Littlefield Publishing Group
4501 Forbes Boulevard, Suite 200, Lanham, Maryland 20706
www.scarecroweducation.com

PO Box 317
Oxford
OX2 9RU, UK

British Library Cataloguing in Publication Information Available

Library of Congress Cataloging-in-Publication Data
Huber, Susan J. (Susan Joanna), 1944–
    The best dressed list : classroom trends and cultural fashions / Susan
J. Huber.
        p. cm.
"A ScarecrowEducation book."
Includes bibliographical references.
    ISBN 0-8108-4627-6 (pbk. : alk. paper)
    1. Educational sociology—United States. 2. Popular culture—
States. I. Title.
LC191.4 .H83 2003
306.43—dc21   2002015097

∞™ The paper used in this publication meets the minimum requirements of
American National Standard for Information Sciences—Permanence of Paper
for Printed Library Materials, ANSI/NISO Z39.48-1992.
Manufactured in the United States of America.

The teacher who is indeed wise
Does not bid you to enter the house of his wisdom
But rather leads you to the threshold of your mind.

—Kahlil Gibran

For Jack, Thomas, and Andrew
Who bring love and joy to my life

Contents

Introduction: Sounding the Alert

In a completely rational society, the best of us would aspire to be teachers and the rest of us would have to settle for something less, because passing civilization along from one generation to the next ought to be the highest honor and responsibility anyone could have.

—Lee Iacocca

Teachers are ordinary people who choose to do extraordinary work. They accept responsibility for preparing students to explore limitless possibilities. This makes their work more critical than most, more rewarding than most, and more difficult than most. Teaching offers no rewards for the faint of heart and sometimes too few for the stalwart. But for those who opt to stand up to the challenge, a chance to remold the world awaits.

I am a teacher of teachers who is curious about how people, in general, and teachers, in particular, make meaning of their work. Each day that I meet with my students, I find opportunities to peel back layers of embedded cultural behavior that highlight who I am as teacher and learner and who they are as teachers and learners. What I uncover energizes me to continue to study the culture of the classroom and to urge my students to do the same.

Years ago, I proudly marched across the stage as an undergraduate student having earned degrees in the liberal arts and secondary education. Six months prior to my graduation, I contractually agreed to teach Latin and English to high school students. I have spent my professional career teaching and learning from preschool-age children to doctoral candidates. Although I cut my educational teeth in secondary education, I also worked as an elementary school principal prior to finding my niche in higher education. My educational background, my teaching experiences, and my own curiosity have made me acutely aware of the roller coaster of emotions associated with teaching and learning that rocks both sides of the desk.

I sometimes wince as experienced teachers in elementary and secondary classrooms introduce bright-eyed education students to their first dose of reality in the classroom. These preservice teachers, who must engage in field experiences as part of their professional education studies, intend to contribute their talents to society by establishing a career for themselves as classroom teachers. They come from a variety of socioeconomic backgrounds and differ as to gender, age, race, and religion; but they all share a common desire to work as educators with and for youth. Reasons they cite for choosing a career in education are obviously personal and multiple, but several are quite typical. Students genuinely interested in scholarship find teaching a natural career path to follow. Some choose the classroom because of teachers they admired, while others love working with children and visualize the classroom as a potter's studio. Some prospective teachers seek the autonomy that teaching offers; some seek a work schedule that at first blush looks inviting; and some few naively seek to restore the profession of teaching to a meaningful status in society, whatever that might be. Regardless of the motivation that folds students into the ranks of teachers, society should be grateful for their interest.

However, teaching, formerly a career field for lifers, now offers short-term career options for too many students. What happens in the classroom to these fresh teachers that causes so many of them to change career paths so quickly? The reality of a K–12 teaching career today is so far afield from the preservice dreams students have of mentoring eager-to-learn children à la "Sir" or "Mr. Holland" or Jaime Escalante[1] that many disillusioned novice teachers leave the field. Trying to convince millennial youth of the requisite need for reflection and critical thinking is surpassed only by trying to convince the American public that the work teachers do in the classroom is as vital to the well-being of the United States as combating terrorism. Society is too eager to grant teachers and their work minimal status. Teachers are not film-star heroes; they don't hold jobs most people would covet; and they don't earn a salary that impresses anyone. Although few citizens would argue with the fact that good teachers are an extraordinarily valuable commodity for society, most would be shocked to think that their own beliefs and behavior contribute to the ongoing demise of the profession.

In reflecting on my own educational career, I realized that one of the reasons I chose to remain in the field was because of my personal interest in studying the everyday behavior of ordinary people from both an experiential and a scholarly perspective. These everyday behaviors, elusive as the air we breathe because of individual scholarly interpretation, swirl around us almost imperceptibly as popular culture. How you interpret life, of course, depends on the lens you use. The theoretical frameworks that have helped inform my own thinking about education in a democratic society have come from educators and philosophers such as John Dewey,[2] Michael Apple,[3] Nel Noddings,[4] and Maxine Greene;[5] from the cultural concepts of social scientists like Clifford Geertz[6] and Roger Keesing;[7] from Harold Blumer's[8] and Erving Goffman's[9] idea of *symbolic interactionism;* and from the cultural critiques of Henry Giroux,[10] Peter McLaren,[11] and others. I am neither an anthropologist nor a sociologist, however. I am an educator who has a practitioner's way of looking at culture. I like to consider culture as "the acquired knowledge people use to interpret experience and generate behavior."[12] As an educator, I gravitate toward this definition of *culture* because it considers aspects of knowledge and behavior with an action component rooted in it. In this way, culture takes on an interactive agenda and fuses what people know with how they use their knowledge to act within their community. I believe culture is inclusive of all that we know and believe and value as people. Culture shapes our behavior, ideas, and emotions. It gives meaning to our way of acting and interacting with others and creates an image of us as people that we respond to both individually and collectively. Thus, culture provides the context for our societal mores and also the rationale for our actions as men and women and teachers in the classroom.

In *The Best Dressed List,* I investigate the intersection of American culture, popular culture, and classroom culture and unpack the effects the mixture has on teachers and students. I concern myself with values endemic to society at large and especially to school-age children and youth, who take for granted growing up with a sense of entitlement, capture world news in sound bites, and shop via the Internet. These same children willingly practice free throws by the hour, but time their reading by the minute; they obsess about weight and body image, but lobby for junk food in the school cafeteria. They run marathons for disease prevention but ignore taking precautions against STDs. Teachers, caught off guard in the midst of clashing values, find themselves forced to compete with popular culture in ways they never imagined.

What teacher education program prepares students to bring the excitement of the big screen to the classroom? How many teachers can command undivided attention from students in the same way as PlayStation2 or communicate information with the speed and intensity of an online instant message? Teachers don't learn these skills in teacher preparation programs and, more to the point, don't learn why they might be important. Anthropology and sociology majors discuss and dissect cultural definitions and theories; education students do not. Popular culture, for me an expression of what people value, continually goes toe-to-toe with education, an institution we also purport to value highly. Teachers find themselves contending with parenting behaviors that hinder learning, societal priorities that place schooling near the bottom of the "to-do list," public mania for instant gratification, MTV, and the like, and they simply aren't prepared for the task.

In the following pages, I aim to contribute to teachers' understanding of culture and praxis by weaving personal narrative and tales from my own classroom experiences and conversations into an examination of the intersection of popular culture and education. Historically, narrative has been a powerful way to construct learning. During the last two decades, the concept of *voice* has been linked to narrative inquiry in education as a way to empower teachers. Giving voice to classroom experiences not only helps teachers to interpret and to better understand their practice, but also to understand who they are as educational leaders. Teachers need to speak and be heard about teaching so that others come to understand teaching as teachers do.[13]

The stories I tell are intended to illuminate experiences I have had in the classroom and not to prescribe a behavioral code. My look at popular culture is to alert teachers, parents, and others interested in the educational process to the growing acceptance of nonchalantly dismissing K–12 classroom education as culturally irrelevant and to provoke them into reflecting on how to alter that perspective. I choose to use personal and professional tales to communicate from my educational world to the larger world, to speak out, to interpret, to inform, and to teach. I believe that understanding popular culture as a process for defining values and as a pedagogical tool for learning can be an invaluable aid to teachers in helping them to reclaim the classroom and their profession.

NOTES

1. Mr. Holland, from the film, *Mr. Holland's Opus,* Sir, from *To Sir with Love,* and Jaime Escalante, made famous in *Stand and Deliver,* are three heroic teachers who, against all odds, win the admiration and respect of their students and colleagues in an idealized educational setting.

2. John Dewey, *The School and Society and the Child and the Curriculum* (Chicago: University of Chicago Press, 1991); *Experience and Education* (New York: Scribner, 1997); *Democracy and Education: An Introduction to the Philosophy of Education* (New York: Simon & Schuster, 1997); *How We Think* (New York: Dover, 1997).

3. Michael Apple, *Official Knowledge* (New York: Routledge, 1993); *Education and Power* (New York: Routledge, 1995); *Cultural Politics and Education* (New York: Teachers College Press, 1996).

4. Nel Noddings, *Philosophy of Education* (Boulder, Colo.: Westview, 1995); *Educating for Intelligent Belief or Unbelief* (New York: Teachers College Press, 2000).

5. Maxine Greene, *The Dialectic of Freedom* (New York: Teachers College Press, 1988); *Releasing the Imagination: Essays on Education, the Arts, and Social Change* (New York: Jossey-Bass, 2000).

6. Clifford Geertz, *The Interpretation of Culture* (New York: Basic, 1973).

7. Roger Keesing and Andrew Strathern, *Cultural Anthropology: A Contemporary Perspective* (London: Wadsworth, 1997).

8. Harold Blumer, *Symbolic Interactionism: Perspective and Method* (Englewood Cliffs, N.J.: Prentice-Hall, 1969).

9. Erving Goffman, *The Presentation of Self in Everyday Life* (New York: Doubleday, 1959); *Interaction Ritual: Essays on Face-to-Face Interaction* (New York: Doubleday, 1967); *Strategic Interaction* (Philadelphia: University of Philadelphia Press, 1969).

10. Henry Giroux, *The Mouse That Roared: Disney and the End of Innocence* (Lanham, Md.: Rowman & Littlefield, 2001).

11. Peter McLaren, *Life in Schools: An Introduction to Critical Pedagogy in the Foundations of Education* (New York: Longman Publishing Group, 1994).

12. James Spradley, *Participant Observation* (New York: Holt, Rinehart & Winston, 1980), 9.

13. Michael Cortazzi, *Narrative Analysis* (London: Falmer Press, 1993).

1

Surviving Popular Culture

Culture is the name for what people are interested in, their thoughts, their models, the books they read and the speeches they hear, their table-talk, gossip, controversies, historical sense and scientific training, the values they appreciate, the quality of life they admire. All communities have a culture. It is the climate of their civilization.

—Walter Lippmann

Friday has been my favorite day of the week for almost as long as I can remember. When I was a young girl, the day generally held a promise of something unexpectedly special. My grandfather, who cashed his weekly paycheck every Friday, used to surprise me with a pack of gum and nickel candy bars. Sometimes my dad would whistle his way in the back door after work and declare it had been a tough week and wonder if anybody wanted to go out for dinner. My grade school teachers saved their most interesting lessons for Fridays because we were restless by then. And by the time I reached high school, I truly understood that life began on Friday. Now, after years of cultural conditioning, I still mentally mutter "TGIF" at the end of the week and hope for something surprising to happen.

On a recent Friday, I wasn't disappointed. I walked into my class titled "Education's Place in Society" a few minutes earlier than usual to get things set up for a simulated debate that was going to take place. My teachers-to-be had just finished reading John Dewey's *Experience and Education*.[1] I intended to bring Dewey into the twenty-first century (casting myself as the venerable Dr. Dewey) to defend his stance on the inadequacy of educational movements that aren't derived from a philosophy of experience. I had used this technique before to show students that Dewey's philosophy is as relevant today as it was in the 1930s. Students usually left class with a new respect for Dewey's philosophy if the simulation was lively enough.

A group of students were in a heated discussion when I came into the room, and they paid little attention to my class preparations. I smiled to myself and nostalgically thought, "Some things never change—it's Friday and they're restless." I listened to snippets of their conversation while I unpacked my briefcase and quickly realized that the only thing Friday had to do with the intensity of their conversation was that it followed Thursday. Apparently, they had all watched Thursday's telecast *Survivor: The Australian Outback* on TV. Kim, a bright, upbeat young woman, was bemoaning the networks' decision to pit CBS's *Survivor* against NBC's *Friends*. I listened to her say, "But everybody knows Thursday night is the most important TV night. It was a greedy marketing decision to run *Survivor* opposite *Friends* during sweeps month. Now I'll have to tape *Friends*." I watched heads nod in agreement. There was no debate on that point.

I glanced around the room as students started filling in the desks, and I mused momentarily about a few things that had changed. David and Andy had their baseball hats on, as usual. I wondered if they were bald. I had never seen either of them without a hat. I gave up asking students to remove hats in the classroom several years ago. It was a losing battle. Men wear baseball hats at work, in restaurants, at wakes, in church—anywhere and everywhere. Why make school an exception? Women wear hats in class too. In fact, Ali, slouched down behind David, was wearing her "bad hair day" hat. Almost everyone was dressed in some variation of jeans and a sweatshirt. It was the unofficial winter uniform. I was silently happy it was February and too cold for shorts and spaghetti-strap T-shirts—one less distraction to confront.

Bulging, black backpacks began cluttering up the aisles. Valerie and Brooke teetered in on chunky-soled shoes with very high heels that made their feet look out of proportion to the rest of their bodies. I hoped they wouldn't trip over somebody's backpack and wondered if they would wear those shoes for student teaching. Robert's cell phone rang, and I must have inadvertently glared. "Class hasn't started yet, man," he mumbled in defense. I refuse to allow students to converse on their phones in my class. I don't look kindly on those who receive calls and move out into the hallway to talk either. I'm not in the least concerned about the correlation between cell phones and cancer, but I am curious about what sort of dependence they breed between users.

Class began, and John Dewey came to life. The students enjoyed this session, as predicted. However, it was Friday afternoon, and when two o'clock rolled around, the students hurriedly left. I was as anxious to leave as they were, but I couldn't let go of the preclass conversation on which I had eavesdropped. I really wanted to discuss TV programming and the merits of *Survivor* with Kim and the others, but I was glad they had hurried off. Nonetheless, I couldn't stop thinking about what makes *Survivor* so fascinating to the general public. I had read in the newspaper that the *Survivor II* telecast garnered 43.6 million viewers nationally for its premiere.[2] The students obviously weren't the only folks buzzing about the program. I was perplexed about what 44 million viewers could find intriguing to watch on that program. Maybe it's just the trendy thing to tune in to so you have something to talk about with your friends? Maybe it's pure escapism? Maybe it's a way to vicariously compete with others in the safety of your living room?

On my drive home, I replayed in my head my newly discovered nugget of knowledge from Kim: "Everybody knows Thursday night is the most important TV night." I didn't know that. One TV night seems as vapid as the next to me. I tried to come to terms with why I was so bothered by my students' interest in a TV program. I understand we all have our favorite pastimes, and watching *Survivor* is not one of mine. I have no interest in watching a leaderless group of people publicly challenge and humiliate one another on TV. I am disgusted by the weekly elimination of a participant that allows the cunning survivor to achieve questionable fame and accrue one million dollars. It reminds me of cruel playground antics for choosing friends. But then, I don't enjoy watching *CNN Live* broadcast juicy scandals in full color or watching onetime celebrities on daytime TV line up to whisper their family secrets for the world to hear either. However, I don't expect my students to watch what I enjoy on television and vice versa.

While mulling this over, I realized it wasn't only the particular program that caused my reaction, it was also the ritualistic importance attached to

setting aside a specific night for what sounded like mandatory TV view-
ing. I was the only person in my classroom who had not watched TV on
the previous night. American society has always had certain activities des-
ignated for specific days, such as live entertainment on Saturday evenings
and family picnics on Sunday afternoons, so this shouldn't be alarming;
but the warning flag was signaling to me. The implied sense of voyeurism
that viewers brought to their conversation about the program was another
thing that I couldn't dismiss. I heard it in Kim's tone of voice and in her
friends' responses. They wouldn't consider missing the weekly episode of
Survivor.

Millions of television viewers, like Kim, are hooked on reality broadcasts such as *Survivor, Temptation Island,* and *Fear Factor.* They seem to
need media producers to interpret the world for them and are eager to buy
into the cheap illusion. Millions of people also find it entertaining to peep
into the personal behavior of individuals or groups, like Ozzy Osbourne's
family, who are willing to have their every movement recorded via a web
camera and flashed on MTV or the Internet. And readers continue to put
"writer-tells-all" exposés on the *New York Times* best-seller book list week
after week. What does this tell us about our popular culture? When the
most prominent TV shows are those that pit human beings against one another for our entertainment, what does this suggest about American values? What does this mean for educators? I realized that *Survivor* was only
the catalyst that propelled me to the real questions I needed to explore, and
I felt invigorated. This Friday's gift was indeed unexpected.

School has been a way of life for me. I have been on one side of the
desk or the other since I entered kindergarten. Today, as a university professor, I teach preservice teachers, full-service teachers, and aspiring principals. I have been privileged to witness and partake in remarkable
changes in schools and in teaching in the last half century. Technology, for
example, has dramatically changed every teacher's life. Going backward
in time, I remember receiving dittoed work sheets in grammar school that
were handwritten by my teachers and frequently smudged in purple ink.
Present-day students would immediately complain about illegible sen-
tences, even though they might enjoy sniffing the paper. As a beginning
teacher, I recall quickly learning how to thread a film through a movie
projector with dexterity so I wouldn't have to ask a smirking AV Club
member in my class for assistance. DVDs give us theaterlike luxury in the

classroom nowadays. I can mentally recall the voices of two school board members chastising me as a principal for asking for a budget modification in 1985 to include new Apple IIE computers for the library. I was told we had better things to spend money on than expensive gimmicks no one would use. Today, libraries have been turned into media centers, and students couldn't imagine working without computers. I couldn't either.

Technology in education provides an obvious example of change, but there are many other less obvious changes that have sneaked up on us. For instance, when did extracurricular activities surpass homework on any student's priority list? Why do so many primary-grade teachers include lessons on how to use silverware in their nutrition units? Why do schools sell condoms in vending machines? When did students stop feeling safe in school? If it is true that schools are the reflecting ponds of society, then the stability or turmoil of one institution must mirror the stability or turmoil of the other.

Schools offer a common threshold for transmitting knowledge, so if there is something that all citizens should learn, the obvious place to have them do so is in school. Years ago, my mother and father both learned to drive as young adults, but certainly not by enrolling in a driver's education class. Their fathers took them to a cemetery (perhaps the somber location was chosen for reasons other than lack of traffic) to practice maneuvering the automobile. In the 1930s, when my grandfather decided my mother was ready to drive his car, she walked to the nearest drugstore and paid twenty-five cents to purchase a license to drive. When cars became commonplace and driving was quickly turning into a free-for-all, society demanded that driving behavior change. Driver's training was relegated to the schools years ago and remains a curricular staple. Drug education, sex education, AIDS education, and multicultural education are similar examples of curricular additions called for by societal change. Societal change acts like an invisible school board member shaping school curricula, policy, and pedagogy. It's here that popular culture and education intersect. Popular culture represents an expression of what we value and hold dear. It is a subset of the larger cultural system that embraces our customs, traditions, values, actions, and interactions. Popular culture is so much a part of our heritage—so ordinary—that we can easily overlook how it embellishes our identity.

A German exchange student asked me one day where he should shop to get the best price on a pair of Nikes. He somewhat sheepishly told me he wanted to look more American on campus. In his mind, Nike must be the trademark of all Americans. I know American tourists abroad are easily identified by their baseball hats and athletic shoes, not exactly garb for the haute couture set, but typically American. Americans aren't about to give up their favorite headgear and footwear when traveling in order to look like someone they aren't. What we wear symbolizes who we are and what we value as much as what we read, what we do with our leisure time, and how we interact with others. Schools, as both institutions of learning and complex human systems, also represent who we are and what we value. When societal values clash with educational values, teachers find themselves competing with popular culture.

At first blush, the teachers-versus-pop culture argument may seem a stretch. The connection, however, is only too overt. Brian's story exemplifies what I mean. One morning, Brian, a faithful class attendee, was absent. At the next class meeting, I mentioned I had missed him during the last class. He told me he just couldn't make it that day because he had been up all night waiting in line to get his son the coveted PlayStation2 for Christmas. Here is a perfect instance of teachers having to compete with pop culture. Brian, a prospective teacher, had to come to terms with his personal priorities. He really disliked missing class, but being consumer savvy, he knew that if he missed this "opportunity," he would disappoint his son. I had to schedule an appointment with Brian after class to discuss what he had missed previously so he could complete an assignment. The fourth-grade teacher of Brian's son will be competing for attention from all of the fourth graders who steep themselves in some version of video mania over the Christmas holidays and come back to school yearning for the same level of entertainment.

What average teacher can plan a curriculum that rivals the hand-gripping excitement of Nintendo games? Whose classroom instruction can claim the same riveted attention that students give to Eminem or Britney Spears? What teacher can charm and disarm day after day in the classroom like Julia Roberts or Tom Hanks? How does a teacher make the argument for teaching Johnny to read when Johnny's parents really believe he has a better chance for success in his future life by perfecting his slap shot? Of course, teachers shouldn't have to be pressured by entertainment trends or sports or multimedia or the marketplace. But they are.

The intersection of education and popular culture is educational reality, and right now, delving into reality is high on the pop culture charts. Besides the reality-TV programs of the *Survivor* genre, television brings us reality-based dramas like *The West Wing* and *ER*, and investigative reporters provide us with shuddering doses of reality on *CSI, 60 Minutes, 20/20*, and the like. Garry Trudeau's comic strip, *Doonesbury*, brilliantly plumbs the depths of political reality; children verbally encourage their classmates to "get real" and tell them how upon occasion; and even some of us in the "ivory tower" seek cultural reality through conducting qualitative research projects.

Reality-based learning is key to education's survival. Teachers cognitively know the importance of connecting classroom learning to students' lives and interests. If they don't, students of all ages are only too quick to ask why they have to learn something they will never use in the "real world." Competing with pop culture isn't the answer for teachers, nor is pandering to a common denominator. There are lessons to be learned from understanding how to link pop culture to pedagogy.

> Culture is ordinary. . . . Every human society has its own shape, its own purposes, its own meanings. Every human society expresses these, in institutions, and in arts and learning. The making of a society is the finding of common meanings and directions, and its growth is an active debate and amendment under the pressures of experience, contact, and discovery writing themselves into the land.[3]

It is the ordinariness of popular culture that interests me. I need to understand its direction and expression in the classroom in order to teach my students and myself how to be "survivors."

NOTES

1. John Dewey, *Experience and Education* (New York: Scribner, 1997).

2. D. Petrozzello, "New York Daily News," *St. Paul Pioneer Press,* February 8, 2001, E6.

3. Raymond Williams, "Culture Is Ordinary," in *Schooling the Symbolic Animal,* ed. Bradley A. U. Levinson, with Kathryn M. Borman, Margaret Eisenhart, Michele Foster, Amy E. Fox, and Margaret Sutton (Lanham, Md.: Rowman & Littlefield, 2000), 32.

2

(Un)Scholarly Trends

Education . . . is a painful, continual and difficult work to be done in
kindness, by watching, by warning . . . by praise, but above all—by
example.

—John Ruskin

It would be decidedly difficult to portray scholarship as chic in American
culture. The popular trend is to downplay the significance of intellectual-
ism and erudition in favor of pragmatism and application. Learning for its
own sake has become the purview of a few scholars in academe who
choose to fashion their lives around their scholarly interests. For the majority of the populace, education is either mandated by statute or directly
linked to earning a credential or degree needed to obtain a job or to ad-
vance in a career field. Education, once a privilege, now reflects little
more than a basic entitlement. Thus, in reductionist terms, education is
simply a means to an end, sandwiched somewhere in between family,
work, recreation, and the real world.

Newspaper and magazine columnists, TV and radio talk show hosts,
state and federal legislators, corporate gurus and blue-collar workers, parents and teachers alike hotly contest and publicly bemoan the benefits and
costs of education and the demands of educators. The debates continue to
underscore the inadequacy of the educational system and promote performance standards as a cure-all. As a result, the public clamors for educational accountability for tax dollars spent. By implication, teachers and

the methodologies they employ become pawns in the published pass/fail statistics that supposedly hold them accountable for what their students have learned. The popular debates, which could be structured as healthy discourse to legitimize the significance of education, generally have the opposite effect. Classroom teachers, seldom participants in the public debates surrounding educational reform, walk a tightrope, but the dilemma they face is as much about an anti-education attitude as it is about reformation of the system.

Recently, I began teaching an off-campus class of adult students who were all principals in the making. We were scheduled to meet in a suburban church hall in a large, lower-level meeting room. The spacious room had typical cafeteria-style tables, and the class coordinator had moved a few of them into a U shape to carve out a specific space for the class. At our very first meeting, I was about halfway through my introductory course comments when someone began rattling the outside door to the church hall. Before anyone could make a move to open the door, the inner double doors to our meeting room swung open with a vengeance. The disruption startled everyone, but it wasn't nearly as startling as the vituperative words that followed. A dour, middle-aged woman, armed with several bolts of fabric and a couple of plastic bags hanging from each arm, lurched her way across the room. In what seemed like less than a nanosecond, she divested herself of the plastic bags and bolts of material. With hands on her hips, she defiantly proceeded to dress us down. "You have no business in here. I don't care who you are, where you're from, or what you're teaching. We have this room for quilting. Get out! Go to the Bride's Room! Go on; just get out!"

Nonplussed for a moment, I thought I had better go directly to the Bride's Room and not look back. However, to stem what I feared might end up to be more than snickering, I immediately announced to the cohort of students that we needed to take a quick break. I literally grabbed the class coordinator, who was an employee of the church, and asked her what to do about this intrusion. She assured me there must be some mistake. She knew the quilt maker and went to an adjacent kitchen to sort things out with her. Ten minutes into the second half of class, we had a repeat performance of the previous incident. This time, a diminutive, young woman stood hesitatingly in the doorway for a moment, only to be hailed in by the previous interloper. The second quilt maker, with only a couple of bags of fabric squares, rudely rustled her way through our space without an "excuse me" or even a glance in our direction. The co-conspirators quickly put their heads together, and the "I told them . . ." phrases wafted across the room as the two of them laughed and talked about the situation as if *we* had interrupted *them*. In my most professional manner, I ignored the two women and continued on with the remnant of my PowerPoint presentation, which seemed to have lost most of its punch.

I assumed this display of childish pique on the other side of the room would die down and decided to press on with the last minutes of class. To my dismay, four more women barged in with bolts and bags of quilting fabric, vigorous door slamming, and a great deal of ballyhoo. The leader of the group regaled each woman separately with the same story we heard initially. By the final iteration, my students were grim faced, the class coordinator was ashen, and I was livid. As I struggled to quickly end class, the quilt makers paid us no mind. They talked over us and set up two sewing machines that whirred noisily away. They began to iron in one corner of the room and willfully banged the iron on the board in a maddening rhythm. The group leader loudly continued to ask if anyone knew why we (jerking her head in the direction of my class) didn't go to the Bride's Room.

The class coordinator assured me the next day that she had scheduled this community room for our class on Wednesdays from 4:30–7:00 P.M. The women who assembled quilts had a long-standing weekly meeting time for Wednesday evenings at 7:30 P.M. Seemingly, there should have been no schedule conflict, but apparently, the foremost quilt maker decided the group had squatters' rights. They always arrived an hour early to set up for the evening. The coordinator thought we could amicably share the room for the overlapped time on that evening of the week and worked out the details for future use, but the women were members of the church on whose property we were holding class; we were not. In their worldview, they were entitled because of membership; we were not. They felt it was their right to dismiss any group who intruded on what they deemed their space—including a group of adults who chose to spend their after-hours time studying to become principals. In short, they attached no value to education.

I pinch myself for a validity check when I revisit that evening in my mind, and then I become indignant about colonization. Why would six

adult women, members of a church community that financially supports a
school and its employees, choose to flex their power as they did? The quilt
makers knew they could claim the room at 7:30 P.M. Why did they insist
on arriving sixty minutes early? They understood the scheduling process
and knew they didn't own the space any more than we did. They played
their priority card when they chose to dominate the space. Education
didn't fit into their value system.

I thought I had previously encountered every type of rudeness afforded
educators. This incident, however, ranks among the foremost. It not only
illuminates the increasing lack of esteem many people hold for teachers,
learning, and the educative process, but also illustrates how people who
are dismissive of education couch their behavior in entitlement and coat it
with incivility.

Unfortunately, every imaginable community, church communities
notwithstanding, includes individuals and groups who think they are entitled to special treatment and special privileges, when, in fact, they are not.
The social condition that produced this attitude of entitlement has deep
historical roots in the United States. The structure of domination grew
from these roots and causes, "a continuum of unjust and depersonalizing
relationships among individuals and among groups."[1] On this continuum,
my simple example of depersonalizing entitlement is at the opposite end
from the virulent examples of depersonalization African American slaves
experienced. However, the augmentation of behavior indicative of an attitude of entitlement is too widespread in society to ignore.

When one person or group acts on the premise that they are entitled, another is unfairly subjugated. This social condition is obviously no longer
limited to dominant majorities with economic wealth and political power.
It is slowly being institutionalized into an accepted cultural pattern of behavior. Educational institutions now routinely confront the dangerous
creep of a pervasive sense of entitlement that I refer to as "Lake Wobe-
gone syndrome."

Garrison Keillor predicted a cultural predisposition to entitlement
years ago when he invented Lake Wobegon. Keillor, creator of imagina-
tive and humorous caricatures of everyday life and ordinary culture on
his live Saturday-night radio broadcasts, made his fictional Midwest
Lake Wobegon a haven for entitlement, "where all the women are

strong, all the men good-looking, and all the children above average."[2] Keillor's bitingly sharp humor generalized the symptoms of Lake Wobegon syndrome.

This syndrome (perhaps better termed an *epidemic*) entitles all students to be above average without requiring any reciprocal scholarly activity on their part. It no longer spares any grade level, but more commonly affects students in middle school on up. Professional educators occasionally refer to this syndrome euphemistically as "grade inflation." The cultural syndrome requires educators to understand that A's are the target grade, B's are acceptable, and anything less than a B has a stigma attached to it. It makes no difference if a rubric indicates that a C is acceptable; it isn't. It's average. Above-average students are entitled to A's and only begrudgingly accept B's.

Lake Wobegon syndrome cyclically runs its course in my academic community. It follows a pattern similar to this: Student X theorizes, "I pay tuition, which is very expensive. This entitles me to receive certain services, such as good instruction that will help me to attain my academic goal, advising when needed, library services, bookstore services, counseling, health, and all the other available student services provided by the academic institution." So far, so good. Student X is generally pleased with the university services until grade reports are posted. Then she finds she has earned one B, two C's, and one D. Enter Student Y, X's friend. He has earned three grades of A and one grade of A–. Student X knows she has studied as hard as her friend Y. Following lengthy conversation with friends and minimal personal reflection, Student X decides she just got stuck with lousy professors who don't know how to teach. Student Y encourages his friend X to talk to her professors. "After all, you're entitled to find out why you received the grades you did." This is good advice, and Student X follows it.

Student X sets up an appointment to meet with Professor Banal. The professor spends an hour with her and goes over her test items. He points out that she seemed to lack a depth of understanding, as evidenced in her once-over-lightly type of responses to several essay questions. He also reminds her of his policy that allows students to retake tests, within a specified time frame, on which they scored poorly. He asks Student X why she never took the opportunity for a retake. Student X sheepishly answers, "The retakes just didn't fit my time schedule." She mutters something inaudible that sounds like "shift working and stuff." She eagerly leaves the office and realizes that she should have followed through on the retakes.

Student X then decides to meet with Professor Knerd, much as she dislikes her. Knerd has the reputation of "buckling" with grades if you really press her, so it's worth the shot. Knerd immediately puts Student X on the defensive by getting directly to the point in her usual irritating manner. She asks her why she never rewrote her first two papers for class. Her notes indicate that on the first and second assignments, Student X received a grade of R (rewrite). Student X listens to Professor Knerd nasally intone, "My records indicate that you chose to keep the two R grades, and that is what impacted your final grade." Student X rather brazenly asks Knerd if she realizes how much time it takes to rewrite her papers (mentally modifying *papers* in this sentence with the word *stupid*). She reminds Knerd that her later papers were B papers and that proves she could do the work. As Student X summons up the courage to request a change in grade, Knerd cuts her off with what sounds like a "we all make choices" lecture. Student X, near tears, rushes out of the office, impudently questioning what she gets for all the tuition she pays.

Strict's office is the last stop. Student X steels herself as Professor Strict matter-of-factly tells her she missed 40 percent of her class and, as a result, didn't fully participate in any of the cooperative group projects. "You can't ride the crest of your colleagues' work for the entire semester and expect an A for their effort, Ms. X. It clearly states in the class syllabus that you cannot make up missed collaborative work." Student X feels a slow burn emerging. Of course she missed some classes. The material was so mundane, she didn't need to attend every class. She could read the text and keep up with the group. She thought she did. When she argued this point with Strict, she lost. Students always lose with Professor Strict.

Humiliated and a bit chagrined, Student X confers with her friends. They advise her to go back to Banal and Knerd and to try to convince them to let her retake the tests and rewrite the papers. They assure her that these two professors are really pretty decent, if you eat humble pie. Strict is another matter, however.

Student X indeed secures her second chance from Banal and Knerd. But Professor Strict explains to Student X how it is simply impossible for her to reproduce the learning circles created over the semester. She reiterates that she stated her policy in the syllabus and discussed it in class on more than one occasion. She adamantly refuses to change the grade. Student X leaves Professor Strict's office in tears. She's fearful she will lose her scholarship if she receives a D, and besides that, her parents will insist she bring her car back home.

Student X goes directly to the dean of students. She explains her situation and informs the dean that she believes she is entitled to improve her grade. She knows Professor Strict dislikes her because she can keep up with the material without wasting all that time on group work; everybody in class knows it. It wasn't her fault that she missed so many classes. When the dean starts to explain the concept of *academic freedom,* it sounds as if he is defending Strict's refusal to let Student X make up the work because she is the professor and it is her right. He asks if she received a syllabus and if she understood how this particular class would be focused on collaborative work groups and graded on collaborative projects. Student X is aware of all this and declares, "Enough is enough." Feeling devastated, she storms back to the dormitory, where her friends encourage her to put her grievance in writing.

Entitlement presupposes that a person should be adequately and fairly authorized something in reciprocation for some activity. With false entitlement, a person presupposes something is due without the reciprocal activity actually taking place. For example, the church quilt makers were entitled to meet in the church-owned room provided they follow the established practice of scheduling the room. They did schedule the room for an appointed time. However, they believed church membership accorded them a special privilege—that of using the room whenever they pleased, regardless of the scheduled time. Membership, in their minds, granted them ownership. Thus, they owned the room; the students were only renters. Their false sense of entitlement diminished any sense of wrongdoing on their part.

Similarly, Student X is entitled to receive an A grade provided she meets the established criteria. Her lackluster performance didn't even measure up to an "acceptable B" in three of her four classes. Nevertheless, she believes paying tuition entitles her to an above-average grade regardless of her performance. She is entitled to at least a B based on her personal criteria for scholarship and what she believes are her capabilities. Her professors are responsible for making this possible.

Lack of civility, unfortunately, becomes a postmodern attachment to this false sense of entitlement. It was demonstrated dramatically by the behavior of the quilting group. In processing this class event as a case study, my research students raised multiple questions relating to causal relationships between the event and the subsequent action. How do benign social interactions prompt rude behavior? How is the feeling of displacement responsible for irresponsible behavior? How are relationships of domination played out in exclusionary behavior within social communities? Has the media's depiction of violence so desensitized people that lack of civility seems trivially unimportant? While this was a meaningful exercise in learning how to frame a research question, what we learned from the actual event was far more valuable. Students determined that this remarkable incident was not an anomaly. Examples of lack of civility in their own schools and classrooms easily rolled off the tip of each educator's tongue. In case after case, the perpetrators who lacked civility defended their behavior with entitlement. This clearly demonstrated to the teachers the degree to which society has lost respect for educators and education.

We asked ourselves why we accepted the uncivil behavior and allowed for its continuation that first evening of class. I offered that I tried to give evidence of education as a collaborative venture within a community. Some said they didn't want to add to the mayhem; others didn't want to lose personal self-respect. We all realized we were in rented space and wanted to model civil behavior.

When I asked what we would have done in a traditional classroom setting, one that places the teacher in a position of power, the conversation took on a different tone. One teacher replied, "I would have addressed the issue of civil communication immediately." Another said, "In my own classroom, I won't tolerate incivility. People aren't entitled to act that way. I would have walked the offenders out of the room or called for assistance." We finally admitted we felt powerless that evening. We bowed to the dominant, bullying quilters and felt conflicted about whether that was the best or worst thing to have done given the temporary nature of the problem.

The discussion dramatized two contrasting points: (1) the power and centrality of the teacher in the classroom and (2) the lack of respect for educators and education endemic to our culture. American society and education have grown into a love/hate relationship that contradicts what our ancestors so painstakingly worked to establish several centuries ago. On the one hand, the public displays great pride in the legislative system that mandates free education for all children; on the other hand, it shows blatant disrespect for the educational process that creates its educated citizenry. The attitude, behavior, and resultant actions of six adult women (staunch members of a community that philosophically and financially supports an elementary school) and of Student X (a college student who pays tuition because she ostensibly believes in the value of education) don't stand in isolation. It has become culturally acceptable, if not trendy in some sets, to publicly "blow off" education and negate the purpose it serves.

The popular media sport of "education bashing" helps contribute to the public disregard for education while bracing up the economy. Evening news anchors scoop the local education highlights in two-minute sound bites; paparazzi scramble for scandalous trivia about teachers dating students; Hollywood producers create moneymaking movies about superhuman classroom heroes who inspire their students to accomplish unbelievable feats; and TV sitcoms, like *Coach* or *South Park,* offer yet another take on the status of education in the public eye. Is it any wonder that society has little respect left for education and/or educators?

The widespread notion that education has bottomed out infiltrates even the youngest students. Last year, I volunteered to be a guest reader in my niece's classroom. On the final day of my reading stint, one of the fourth graders asked me if it was true that I was a college teacher. I assured this little girl that indeed it was true. She then turned to my niece, who, until that moment, was beaming with pride at her aunt, and smugly said, "My mom has a really important job. She works downtown and makes a lot of money." As my niece's chin started to quiver, the classroom teacher quickly intervened, with loving care. She deftly thanked me for introducing her fourth graders to *The Secret Garden,*[3] asked my niece to take a bow for supplying the guest reader, and reminded her students that they each were responsible for saying something kind to a classmate today.

Nel Noddings, philosopher and educator, who sees caring as an essential characteristic for effective teaching, addresses civility in the classroom as a teacher's "response-ability."[4] She would have beamed at the quick response of the fourth-grade teacher to my niece and the rest of the students. Lack of civility is a tension-filled issue that educators need to address in the classroom. It is tangled up with a web of entitlement that society lays on teachers' tables to sort out. Noddings speaks of the dual need for teachers to care about their students and to teach them to care about others. Caring teachers have to be able to respond to both the academic needs and the moral needs of their learners so that they teach students to live meaningful lives in concert with others.[5] This "response-ability" of teachers never gets measured in the benchmark exams, nor is it reported in the pass/fail statistics.

I left the fourth graders mentally juxtaposing our postmodern world with that of the ancient Greeks. Aristotle believed that if the city-state taught free, young boys to be "virtuous," they would grow up to be morally responsible citizens. Inculcating values in children would thus create the best possible opportunity for all Greek citizens to live the good life.[6] If Aristotle's philosophy were actually inclusive of all children, we would do well to heed his advice. Nevertheless, the majority of Americans seek the millennial version of Aristotle's beliefs. They believe all children should be taught values needed to live in a democratic society, but what values and who should teach them are undecided questions. No one disagrees that the best possible opportunity to continue the good life lies with the next generation, but education in the "polis" of the ancient Greeks was a far cry from education in America that attempts to prepare students for a democratic way of life. Teachers find themselves caught betwixt and between traditional beliefs and contemporary values. Their reply to the paradox must be to prove that education is infinitely more than a means to an end. Teachers need to re-vision learning as a joyful awakening. Education is the best hope we have to teach people how to live together and creatively explore the possible world. In turn, the public needs to recast education as essential nourishment for the collective mind and spirit of the people. This is the entitlement children deserve.

NOTES

1. Robert J. Starratt, *The Drama of Leadership* (London: Falmer Press, 1993), 64.

2. Garrison Keillor, *A Prairie Home Companion* (St. Paul: Minnesota Public Radio, 1974).

3. Frances Hodgson Burnett, *The Secret Garden* (New York: Children's Classics, 1987).

4. Nel Noddings, "Caring and Competence," in *The Education of Teachers: Ninety-Eighth Yearbook of the National Society for the Study of Education: Part I,* ed. Gary A. Griffin (Chicago: University of Chicago Press, 1999), 216.

5. Noddings, "Caring and Competence."

6. J. A. K. Thomson, trans., E. V. Rieu, ed., *The Ethics of Aristotle* (Baltimore: Penguin, 1963).

3

Confronting the "Isms"

And so our mothers and grandmothers have, more often than not anonymously, handed on the creative spark, the seed of the flower they themselves never hoped to see—or like a sealed letter they could not plainly read.

—Alice Walker

In the opening few minutes of the popular cult movie *Ferris Bueller's Day Off,* Matthew Broderick, starring as the indomitable Ferris, comes out of the shower musing about some "isms" that he knows will be included on the history test he intends to miss on his self-imposed day off. He says, "'Isms,' in my opinion, are not good. A person should not believe in an 'ism.' He should believe in himself."[1] Although Ferris Bueller's casual assessment leaves much ground uncovered, several "isms" that beleaguer teachers and nullify students in the classroom fall smartly into Bueller's "not good" category. While students learn about the intricacies of communism, socialism, fascism, and a host of other "isms" as they uncover history, the stumbling block for teachers lies with confronting racism, sexism, and classism in the classroom.

In spite of desegregated schools and legislation aimed at gender-fair education,[2] racism, sexism, and classism fuel inequities in education just as they do in society at large. These troublesome "isms" inextricably join hands with an inherent belief that posits the superiority of one group over all others. When one race, one sex, or one class of people perceives they

21

are superior, their actions toward those they consider inferior inevitably result in discriminatory behavior. Statistically, the dominant majority of Americans identify themselves as white, which generally equates to claiming western and northern European ancestry.[3] Although the predominant culture in the United States remains that of the majority, the racial makeup of the nation is rapidly changing. "By 2056 most Americans will trace their descent to 'Africa, Asia, the Hispanic world, the Pacific Islands, the Arabic nations—almost anywhere but white Europe.'"[4] This shift in population forces us all to recognize race and ethnicity in new ways in the United States.

Inside of classrooms across the country, teachers engage in an ongoing struggle to meet the needs of students of various cultures, while outside of classrooms, many white Americans still react negatively to a racially diverse America. We have to think back no further than the Rodney King incident and resultant riots in Los Angeles to recognize that racial discrimination in American society often takes an overt form of verbal harassment and physical violence. In many school districts, racial discrimination is covert, especially in schools that serve predominantly poor and nondominant classes of people, resulting in inequities in funding, inadequate facilities, large class sizes, limited instructional materials, outdated technology, and insufficient remedial services. Most destructive of all is the inequity of expectation regarding minority student achievement. Bias of this nature tells us that many Americans see poor and minority students as inferior and not worth the time, effort, and funding afforded predominantly white schools.[5]

Many teachers work hard to challenge the devastating effects of racial bias and to increase self-esteem and academic achievement for all students. One such remarkable teacher, who has been teaching for many years at an urban high school in St. Paul, Minnesota, uses a theatrical format to call attention to the blatant racism her students experience in school. She coaches the students to write reflectively and poetically about issues and situations that are part of their daily lived experience and then helps them to wrap their ideas into a realistic, in-your-face drama. By reflecting on, vocalizing, and dramatizing their feelings, these students attempt to come to terms with issues like being considered a remedial student on the basis of skin color.

The plays produced in this class illustrate that the discriminatory behavior of peers causes heartache for some students. Others address identity confusion and feelings of alienation when they are forced to choose one race over another when filling out school forms on which they fit in multiple categories. They ask, "Why is it that official forms insist people check one box to identify themselves categorically as 'Asian', 'Black', 'Caucasian', 'Hispanic', 'Native American', or 'Pacific Islander'?" Some young men poignantly portray how it feels to watch women clutch their purses and hurry by them because they're black and wear baggy pants. And a few speak of being white in this class, populated almost entirely with minority students, and wonder how this class applies to them.

The much-beloved Caucasian teacher, who levels the playing field for her students in one class for one year, takes her theater troupe on the road to present at conferences, meetings, school district events, and wherever they might be invited. The passionate rap-type poems of her sixteen- and seventeen-year-old students creep into their audiences' psyche, and their performances pique the viewers to question their own attitudes toward race. By caring for her students, their lives, and the world we live in, this teacher helps teenagers render their world manageable. Her students praise her as a teacher who cares for them and their lives. They say she "gets personal," and they mean that in the best imaginable way.

Sexism causes added distress in the classroom. By the time children march off to school, they already are seeing the world through a specific lens informed by familial attitudes, values, and beliefs. Consider the gender patterns in the Green family, for example, with five-year-old Seth and six-year-old Alissa. Seth's parents sign him up to play peewee hockey but cajole his sister, Alissa, who prefers skating to almost any other activity, into taking dance lessons. By making this decision, the family has laid down ground rules for gender stereotyping. Purchasing a Fisher-Price computer game for Seth for his birthday and a Barbie dollhouse for Alissa for her birthday lends further support to the familial gender patterns. Establishing gender-specific chores so that Alissa can learn from her mother in the kitchen and Seth can work with his father out in the yard helps to firmly cement the gender-specific patterns for these two siblings. As Seth gets on the bus for his first day in kindergarten, his father says, "Be sure to answer loudly, son. Go get 'em, Seth." He hugs Alissa and says, "You look cute as a bug, honey. Remember to be a good girl."

In school, the stereotyping lessons continue. Seth answers loudly, as directed, and often. He quickly learns that his teacher will always call on him if he enthusiastically waves his hand in the air. Seth enjoys responding in class because he receives praise for doing so from his teacher. Alissa, remembering to be a "good girl," doesn't always wave her hand in the air to answer. She thinks other children in her class should also have a turn. It bothers Alissa that her teacher forgets her name sometimes and calls her Ashley. She wonders why her teacher can always remember the boys' names. Seth and Alissa have the same lunch period and recess time, but boys and girls sit at separate lunch tables. Boys and girls also play separate games on the playground. Seth plays games with the available sports equipment and runs with the boys; Alissa and her friends play the game four square and learn to stay out of the boys' way. Seth uses the same beginning reader that Alissa used last year when she was in kindergarten. He looks at the picture of a boy and his big brother raking leaves and their sister watching. He sees a picture of a man driving a car with a woman passenger. Seth doesn't realize it yet, but he will see more pictures of boys than of girls, more pictures showing boys in action poses and girls watching, and more pictures of white people than of people of any other color.[6]

Scholars, curriculum specialists, and textbook publishers have joined hands to try to eradicate racism and sexism from textbooks, but this academic cleansing has done little to eliminate either problem. Elementary teachers still face teaching reading from outdated textbooks that promote racial and gender inequity. And secondary English and history teachers (especially) find themselves forced to seek supplementary instructional material if they want to include women and people of color in literature and historical events. These conditions continue to set both women and people of color apart as add-ons, thus reinforcing both gender and racial stereotypes.

A European American, middle-class perspective continues to undergird the curriculum in most schools, which excludes the perspective of women and of poor and minority students. To stop reinforcing the "isms" hidden in curricular materials, teachers (even those fortunate enough to use updated textbooks) must consciously teach students to become critical thinkers so they can separate fact from fiction and put facts into a contextual setting. For instance, if a teacher uses a new textbook that presents re-visioned history to correct historical inaccuracies, the text may still present historical facts in isolation from their social context.[7] For example, it is culturally appropriate that history texts no longer include pictures of what appear to be bloodthirsty American Indians scalping white women and children journeying west in covered wagons. However, if the text fails to address the social context of the westward expansion of the United States in light of the Native Americans or fails to discuss the ethical implications of the movement, it is still promulgating racism. Similarly, including Sandra Cisneros's *The House on Mango Street*[8] on the required English reading list won't necessarily create a feeling of inclusion and worth for young women or Latino students simply because of the listing. Teachers need to affirm cultural diversity by building collaborative relationships with their students, the parents of their students, and community members and by working with them to confront racism, sexism, and classism in the classroom. The goal for all teachers is to have their students achieve success. This is possible only if teachers and students join together to defeat the "isms".

Popular media works hard to promote negative "isms" and plays an enormous role in loading up the public with prejudicial images about the others. Television jump starts the process and subtly teaches children how to stereotype race and gender and continues to reinforce it through adulthood. For example, after a few weekends of fall football broadcasts, one could easily assume that African Americans go to college to play football. A little channel surfing raises the question of why programs featuring Latino stars are broadcast only in Spanish or only on cable TV. Tune in to *The Sopranos,* and it's easy to imagine that all Italians are mobsters; or escape to *Ballykissangel* and believe that the Irish spend most of their waking hours drinking in pubs. If your taste is for classic reruns, *Hogan's Heroes* still shows crafty U.S. soldiers continually outsmarting bumbling German men and women.

Watching a few episodes of *Baywatch* or the parodical *Son of a Beach*— supports the criticism leveled at the American media for being obsessed with sex. These shows and others, such as *Sex and the City* and *Dawson's Creek,* do their best to convince young girls that the combination of a pretty face, a statuesque figure, and sexy clothes is what life is all about.

All in the Family, the most-watched television show in the United States
for a decade spanning the 1970s and 1980s, raised a misogynistic racist to
hero status. Fans waited breathlessly for Archie's bigoted quips week after week. Audiences across the country howled with laughter when Archie
said, "I'll tell you one thing about Nixon. He keeps Pat home. Which was
where Roosevelt should have kept Eleanor. Instead, he let her run around
loose, until one day she discovered the colored. We never knew they were
there. She told them they were getting the short end of the stick and we've
been having trouble ever since."[9] Some folks laughed because they
agreed, and many others laughed for all the wrong reasons. They are still
laughing at the reruns.

People who catch the news through the eyes of their local television
network see pictures of criminals, profiled on a daily basis, with a dispro-
portionate number of minority faces. They connect welfare recipients and
prostitutes with black women, gang members with Asian men, and mi-
grant workers with Hispanics. Thirty-second sound bites that constitute
the news items that explain the visual image do little to allay any precon-
ceived notions a viewer might have about race, gender, or class.

Hollywood also does its part to champion cultural racism with such
blockbuster films as *The Godfather* and Jackie Chan's *Rush Hour.* Other
films like *Whiteboyz, Boyz 'N the Hood, American History X, Falling
Down,* and *Men of Honor* add to the formation of racial stereotypes. Sexism is so rampant in the movie industry that it's difficult not to critique almost any movie for focusing too much attention on cleavage and high
heels, but well-known examples such as *Pretty Woman* and *Coyote Ugly*
easily drive home the point.

Billboards, designed to catch attention, show a stratified world of primarily white faces, scantily clad women, and consumer goods that separate the "haves" from the "have-nots." Popular rap artists like Snoop
Doggy Dogg and Insane Clown Posse denigrate women in song; slick
magazine covers on *Maxim* or *Vogue* or *Cosmopolitan* exploit women;
newspaper ads pander to the middle and upper classes; and on and on.
Considering this sort of media bombardment, it's pointless to question
how society perpetuates racism, sexism, and classism.

We all tote personal baggage packed with positive and negative attitudes toward persons of different racial and ethnic backgrounds, classes,
religions, genders, ages, languages, abilities, and so forth. Teachers come

to school with their cultural beliefs, racial prejudices, gender stereotypes, and class values just as the students do. No one is exempt. The task for teachers is to recognize what discriminatory beliefs they have stowed in their assorted schoolbags and to learn to discard what constitutes racist and exclusionary thinking and behavior, gender bias, and class elitism. Then they can begin teaching their students to see "the others" as the same.

It took me a decade or more of teaching to realize what I had stuffed in my own attitudinal bag, and I'm still unpacking it. I didn't grow up having friendships with any African American, Native American, Asian, or Latino children. My playmates were white, even though I grew up in an inner-city neighborhood. My neighborhood was rich with western European immigrants, ethnic tongues, traditions, foods, and white faces. The culture I embraced was post–World War II American, and, even though I was familiar with many "old-world" customs, I was usually embarrassed to share any cultural differences that were part of my upbringing with my friends from more contemporary families. On my home turf, I enjoyed ethnic food, gleefully participated in the shivarees[10] for neighborhood weddings, and twirled around to live polka music at the neighborhood playground's summer festivals. I accepted my cultural heritage, enjoyed it, and kept it relatively private.

My maternal grandfather, with whom I had the privilege to live during my childhood, spoke English with a German accent and dropped the English altogether whenever his friends came to visit. I loved to listen to the old men talk during those visits because of the passion in their voices, even though I couldn't understand them. My grandfather believed children were to be seen and not heard, so I knew better than to ever interrupt his conversations, but I would ask my mother what they were talking about. I recall her laughing and telling me she couldn't understand everything they said anymore and then giving me the gist of the conversations. Of course, even then, I realized I had no way of knowing if she was actually telling me what she understood or if she was sugarcoating it for my benefit. Among many topics of conversation, these immigrant men spoke often about war and politics.

My grandfather immigrated to America in the early 1900s to escape military conscription in Austria. He had been conscripted once and served unhappily in the military. When he was about to be conscripted a second time, his grandmother gave him money for passage to America to make a life for himself in the United States. Many of his immigrant friends left their homelands and came to the United States for similar reasons. Often when my grandfather's brother-in-law came to visit, the two of them would tell war stories and talk of the Turks. I knew because of the way they almost spat out the word that the Turks must have been terrible enemies in some border skirmish with which they were both too familiar. My great-uncle Peter (my grandfather's brother-in-law) always sat with one leg forward because of a brutal scar on his leg from a Turkish saber. One day, I summoned up enough courage to ask him to show me his scar. To my utter surprise, he did. I had never met a Turk then, and, after seeing my uncle's leg, I was content to keep it that way. This was my introduction to ethnic racism. I had no way of knowing then that someday as a teacher I would come face-to-face with a classroom of "Turks."

My ancestral story parallels the familiar stories of many European immigrant families who came to America around the turn of the twentieth century. My grandfather came to America chasing a dream for peace and prosperity. He grew up very comfortably as a child in Austria, the son of a vintner who owned property and horses, but due to the ravages of war, his family lost their land, their home, and their pride. He worked his entire life in the United States as an unskilled laborer in search of his American dream.

People of a variety of races and cultures traversed oceans to come to America. Some came involuntarily as indentured servants and slaves; some came as laborers. They dreamed of freedom and a better life as they crossed borders and literally built multicultural America. All of us enjoy an infinitely better life because of the boundaries immigrants stretched seeking their dreams. Today, we continue to struggle, both internally and externally, to live together in what Gloria Anzaldua terms a "borderland,"[11] a place where cultures touch and races share common ground.

Elementary and secondary schools have assumed a "borderland" status in the twenty-first century. In schools where cultures touch and races share common ground, they function as immigration stations, of a sort, that mandate that children check in and learn about multiple cultures and races and try to form some common understandings with children different from them. If teachers know how to address the differences and focus on the commonalties people share, then they can successfully guide the twenty-first-century pioneers in peacefully settling the borderlands.

Metaphorically, these borderlands still have trigger-happy guards at the crossing points. Classroom teachers, left to deal with the guards and border crossings, can carefully guide their students into new territory only if they confront the "isms" themselves. The confrontation begins with teachers "unlearning" debilitatingly harmful ideologies that they have been taught both inside and outside of school. Although discarding values we have grown up with is easier to discuss than accomplish, teaching has a built-in ritual, by virtue of its cyclical nature, that aids this process. Teachers begin fresh each fall and have an opportunity to wipe the slate clean each spring. Many teachers say this is one of the more compelling reasons for choosing to teach, discerning that few, if any, other careers allow you an annual new beginning. The renewal ritual can act like a healing restorative, for instance, for teachers who try to learn about racial and cultural beliefs from their students and bury old assumptions. If teachers embed time for honest reflection in the process, it will also help them face the diurnal task of repairing children tattered by cultural norms that have excluded them from the mainstream. The question teachers need to consider is whether or not they have created an equitably positive environment for learning for everyone in their classrooms. If the answer is an unabashed "yes," then the teacher has successfully taken steps to confront racism, sexism, and classism.

Challenging the trend to oversimplify everything of value you have learned to lessons from kindergarten or your mother, I will resist this type of oversimplification. I believe I owe my own confrontation of the "isms" to the Turks (and a few other international students). Years after I learned that the Turks were wartime enemies of my relatives, I found myself outnumbered by students from the Middle East in my classroom. They, of course, had no way of knowing they were my bogeymen. During the time I was transitioning from teaching in the K–12 system to the college classroom, English as a Second Language (ESL) programs began to proliferate on college campuses to accommodate the influx of international students. I, like many other former high school English teachers, found a job teaching ESL to some of these international students.

I marched into my first class as a young, inexperienced ESL teacher not quite sure what to expect. I met fifteen students from the Middle East: Turkey, Iran, Iraq, Jordan, and other Mediterranean countries. We didn't speak one another's language; we didn't understand one another's culture.

We exchanged names and countries of origin and circumspectly eyed one another. The students spoke in halting English, and I was embarrassed that I couldn't understand them very readily. There were two women in the class, who acted mysteriously aloof, and thirteen men, who acted as if they owned the college.

After a few weeks, I noted that the women always sat together in the back row of the classroom, and the men answered for them if they deliberated for a second too long. The women ignored these interruptions at first and then, to my dismay, simply shut down. The men sat in twos and threes and laughed and spoke in their native tongues, whenever possible. They dominated our simple class discussions and intentionally steered the conversation away from the canned textbook conversations to whatever pleased them. Trying to maintain control of the curriculum taxed my skills. Even though I tried to convince myself I was making a little progress with teaching basic English communication skills, the classroom experience for all of us was far from rewarding. The best (or worst) conversational interactions always occurred when I returned graded papers. Grades at least seemed to generate focused conversation. Near the end of the semester, however, when two of the men waylaid me on my way to the parking lot and offered me gold earrings in return for a passing grade, reality clicked in.

I was fearful of those foreigners who didn't respond to me in class in the same way as American students did. I was frustrated with my newly discovered inadequacy as a teacher, and I was very eager to end the semester. I needed to wipe the slate clean. During my own renewal ritual between semester classes, I realized that I had to personally deal with my attitude toward "the Turks" in order to believe in myself (as Ferris Bueller would say) and also to believe in my students.

I greeted the returning ESL students for the second session determined to establish a classroom relationship with them. The men quickly started rearranging the desks I had arranged in a circle. When I refused to allow them to change the arrangement, they complained to the ESL director about the room arrangement. I knew then that I was on the right track.

My agenda included teaching the students to value one another and me as equal partners in the classroom, to listen critically to everyone's words and comments with an intent to learn, and to add English to their repertoire of languages through the use of appropriate linguistic methods. I sat with the students to model my expectations and to both literally and figuratively look "the Turks" in the eye.

Together, as we maintained silence to process responses and as we began to experiment with expanding vocabulary, we nudged the barriers and learned from and about one another. The sexist tier of men seated in front of the women couldn't occur in a circle formation. I concentrated on including the women in our conversation on equal terms, and the men eventually stopped interrupting them. Although some of the students came from families of means, they learned money wouldn't buy a passing grade in class.

We fared far better socially and academically in "ESL II" than I imagined we would. I taught observation skills and listening skills and communication skills, and I learned that I needed to pay strict attention to overtly subduing the "isms". The more conscious we became of one another as human beings, the more we communicated. The classroom dynamic improved proportionately with the language skills. I taught the students English, and they gave me a framework on which to build a theorem for a pedagogical process. After I discarded the notion of teaching them as "others" in the classroom, it was easy to connect language study to the lives and culture of the individual students.

Now a seasoned veteran in the university classroom, I purposefully recollect my ESL days as I meet new students each term. It helps me to create an environment in which my students and I can learn experientially from each other and unlearn some of what's damaging to the human spirit. The challenge grows increasingly more difficult, and I don't always meet it as fully as I would wish. However, I now have a process for helping my students cross the borders, thanks to the ESL students who never received credit for what they taught me. I learned to confront racism and sexism and a host of other negative "isms" by using the basic methodology employed in qualitative research to assist me in systematically exploring the richness of diversity. I tried to make the unfamiliar familiar by connecting the classroom curriculum to students' lived reality. It is a process for confronting the "isms" that fosters pedagogy of understanding and respect. It also allows teachers to connect their everyday practice to research—an added bonus for all those teachers who question the value of studying inquiry as a mandatory requirement for the classroom.

Qualitative inquiry asks the researcher to find patterns of meaning in the behavior of others who think and act and speak differently from what the researcher and others might understand or be comfortable with accepting. This method of inquiry encourages us to understand others on their own terms. As the educator and author bell hooks says,

> To educate for freedom, then, we have to challenge and change the way everyone thinks about pedagogical process. This is especially true for students. Before we try to engage them in a dialectical discussion of ideas that is mutual, we have to teach about process.[12]

Teachers who find occasions to narrow the chasm between in-school life and after-school life need to look beyond curricular content. They need to construct a framework for learning that links curricular content, cognitive and affective learning strategy, and research strategies to the students they teach. They need to validate the importance of personal experience, to teach students how to see one another as human beings sharing a common land, and to teach students how to listen to one another's words, ideas, hopes, and dreams. Because both students and teachers bring their own interests and experiences to the classroom, they make assumptions about what constitutes the experiences of the others and operate from the framework of the assumptions they create. For example, teachers from an upper-middle-class background bring their values to the classroom, and the promulgation of upper- and middle-class values in the classroom continues to silence students from disadvantaged backgrounds. Thus, deconstructing one's personal grid is the first step in the process of learning to value differences.

The basic methodology for qualitative inquiry is deceptively simple. Qualitative researchers learn to gather data by participating in naturalistic observation, conducting interviews, and analyzing documents. As qualitative researchers soon learn, collecting data is interesting, exhilarating, and labor intensive. Data collection is only the beginning of the process, however. Once you understand something about your topic from your data collection, you need to analyze your data to make inferences and make sense of it as if you were seeing it from the vantage point of the other or the studied. Using the same process as researchers do, teachers and students can learn about the others in the classroom from their point of view.

The first step is for teachers and students to become enlightened observers. The process begins with students and teachers looking through multiple lenses at one another as they learn to care for one another in the classroom.

For me, confronting the "isms" is an ongoing process that requires high energy and constant grooming. Once I accepted that I needed to unpack my own bag before I could start chipping away at racism, sexism, and class elitism in my classes, I moved into a borderland. Teachers, prepared or not prepared, must serve as cultural mediators not only for immigrant students who have language and cultural differences, but also for Native American students, African American students, and Latino students who come from families who have lived in the United States for generations. The United States has been a multiracial country since its inception. Lady Liberty still proudly offers to embrace the "tired . . . poor . . . huddled masses yearning to breathe free, the wretched refuse . . . the homeless."[13] Teachers must do no less.

NOTES

1. *Ferris Bueller's Day Off,* Paramount Pictures, 1986.

2. Title IX of the Educational Amendments of 1972, a landmark civil rights law, mandated equal opportunity for females and males in public schools and higher education. Title IX specifically states, "No person in the United States shall, on the basis of sex, be excluded from the participation in, be denied the benefits of, or be subject to discrimination under any, education program or activity, receiving federal assistance." U.S. Department of Education, "Title IX: 25 Years of Progress," 1987, at http://www.ed.gov.pubs/TitleIX, (accessed June 21, 2002).

3. According to the 2000 U.S. census, 75.1 percent of U.S. citizens identified themselves as white (U.S. Bureau of the Census, at www.census.gov/population, 2002 [accessed June 21, 2002]).

4. Ronald Takaki, *A Different Mirror* (Boston: Little, Brown, 1993), 2.

5. Jonathan Kozol, *Savage Inequalities: Children in American Schools* (New York: Crown, 1991).

6. Myra Sadker and David Sadker, *Failing at Fairness: How America's Schools Cheat Girls* (New York: Scribner, 1994).

7. American Association of University Women, *How Schools Shortchanged Girls: The AAUW Report: A Major Study of Findings on Girls and Education* (New York: Marlowe & Co., 1995).

8. Sandra Cisneros, *The House on Mango Street* (New York: Vintage, 1991).

9. Quoted in Deborah Locke, "Civil Discord's Flow," *St. Paul Pioneer Press,* June 28, 2001, A17.

10. A *shivaree* (also called a *charivari*) is a noisy serenade to newlyweds. In our neighborhood, the children would gather pans, pails, and horns of any sort and march to the house of the bride. They would beat on the pans and blow on the horns until the bride appeared. The bride would throw coins to the serenading children, who would then stop the serenade and chase after the scattered coins.

11. Gloria Anzaldua, *Borderlands, La Frontera: The New Mestiza* (San Francisco: Aunt Lute Books, 1987).

12. bell hooks, *Teaching to Transgress* (London: Routledge, 1994), 144.

13. Taken from the inscription engraved on the Statue of Liberty from the sonnet "The New Colossus," written by Emma Lazarus in 1883 and reproduced in part here:

"Give me your tired, your poor,
Your huddled masses yearning to breathe free,
The wretched refuse of your teeming shore.
Send these, the homeless, tempest-tost to me,
I lift my lamp beside the golden door!"

4

Goods-R-Us

From the 1890s on, American corporate business, in league with key institutions, began the transformation of American society into a society preoccupied with consumption, with comfort and bodily well-being, with luxury, spending, and acquisition, with more goods this year than last, more next year than this. American consumer capitalism produced a culture almost violently hostile to the past and tradition, a future-oriented culture of desire that confused the good life with goods. It was a culture that first appeared as an alternative culture—or as one moving largely against the grain of earlier traditions of republicanism and Christian virtue—and then unfolded to become the reigning culture of the United States.

—William Leach

If you poll education students about why they are studying to become teachers, few, if any, would indicate that they choose to teach because of the highly competitive nature of the profession. In fact, most choose to work in the service sector for just the opposite reason: to avoid the cutthroat nature of the corporate world. The cultural quest for acquisition in the United States, however, adds a new dimension to teachers' work. Twenty-first-century teachers surprisingly find themselves hotly competing in a dog-eat-dog career as they contend with the marketplace in unexpected ways. Challenged by parents who seek to give their children every conceivable advantage and by children who are bored with life, teachers find it difficult to create a venue that measures up to what the marketplace has to offer.

The visual world we live in exudes images of colorful, sensual, eye-appealing goods, available seven days a week—goods that tempt us and tease us and beg us to make a purchase. A single click on the BUY IT icon on Netscape.com opens up a plethora of shopping opportunities. From the comfort of home, the inveterate shopper can pursue HOT PRODUCTS, TODAY'S SPECIALS, FEATURED STORES, or, if time is running short, FIND A GIFT for a special occasion. With a few extra clicks, you can send flowers to a loved one across the country, order everything you need to build a quality home-theater system, or cast your vote in the poll for the most important seasonal fashion essential. Daily newspapers delivered to doorsteps across the country feature full-page ads encouraging health-conscious grocery shoppers to use their credit cards to buy everything from artichokes to zinc supplements. Cleverly, catchy TV commercials (like those featuring the Budweiser beer frogs), designed to burn a brand name into the consumer's psyche, capture as much attention as the programs they sponsor and are frequently more entertaining. And Marshall Field's, a major department store chain in the Midwest, even shares with drivers the metaphysical secret of how to "Experience Heaven." Their gigantic billboard on a metropolitan thoroughfare gives you visual directions on this age-old query. A woman climbing the escalator to shoppers' heaven apparently achieves nirvana through "the sheer joy of shopping." Advertising in America draws consumers into the competitive world of the Joneses—that perfect, imaginary world of those who have everything. It also helps to create America's classist society.

Advertising, designed for mass appeal, offers a taste of fantasy for everyone and urges people to step up to what they construe to be the good life. The everyday cook, for instance, admires the colorful fajitas in the restaurant commercials on TV, and, in a moment of gastronomic escapism, drops a red and a yellow pepper (at three times the price of a green pepper) into the shopping basket. The splash of extra color promises to upgrade an ordinary meal into a gourmet dinner. Clothes-conscious consumers hunt in outlet malls in every state across the nation for designer labels that ooze prestige. Similarly, the typical American driver opts for a gas-guzzling SUV, so loaded with extras that it barely needs a driver, even if it's not in the budget. We are a product-oriented people heavily influenced by the media to buy more than we need, and we are largely content with our overconsumption.

Children intuitively understand the concept of *materialism* years before they learn to count money in school, much less recognize its value. Toddlers coyly use smiles and tears to finesse their parents into purchasing all types of consumable goods for them. A common ploy is to bargain for food while grocery shopping. Children momentarily agree to almost anything, if they can just have whatever the commercials, sandwiched in between episodes of *Barney & Friends* and *Arthur,* tout. And they also intuitively understand that plastic cards are a unit of exchange for goods.

American Demographics credits four- to twelve-year-olds with being responsible for $500 billion in household spending in 1997.[1] Psychologist David Walsh tells us that America's advertising industry now looks at three-year-olds as viable consumers.[2] My son verified the horror of this for me when he was two months shy of his third birthday. He brought me a glitzy mail-order catalog, featuring toys to make the mouth water, and pointed out all the things he thought he should find under the Christmas tree. When I suggested to him that perhaps he would find two or three of the many toys he had selected under the tree on Christmas morning, he adamantly assured me that Santa would bring him everything. I tried to turn the conversation into a preschool lesson on values. I introduced him to the legendary St. Nicholas and the origin of gift giving at Christmastime. We formulated a plan, and he agreed that he should pick out the three toys that he would enjoy the most and ask Santa for only those. He selected his three favorites, and that was that. I felt smugly pleased about exposing the crassly commercial aspect of the holiday to my almost three-year-old by using a storytelling method that he enjoyed and accepted. The next day, he brought me the same catalog with a credit card from my purse and asked me to order up all the toys Santa wouldn't be bringing. The situation is not unique, I'm afraid, nor is the desire to acquire whatever greets the eye limited to children.

The concept of *dispose and restock* has emerged from America's preoccupation with materialism. People assess their prominence and popularity by what they dispose of and purchase. The throwaway generation guiltily recycles plastic and glass containers, aluminum and tin cans, and newspapers while they purchase disposable diapers for their infants, juice boxes for their preschoolers, and individually packaged fast food for the whole family. No-longer-new items become tainted by age alone and need to be disposed of and replaced with brand-new items. The term *brand-new* alone carries an implication of better quality solely because of newness.

New is regarded as superior to *used* whether one is talking about consumable goods, cars, clothes, or school buildings. The particularly feminine fetish for up-to-date fashion provides an excellent example of consumers' lust for the latest. If last season's must-have sweater had to be butter-cream yellow, because the luscious color looked almost edible, its fashion luster quickly fades when this season's color turns to a spunky, kiwi green. Typically, the current season's pick replaces last year's next-to-new garment. Fashion advisers constantly urge consumers to clear their closets of any items they haven't worn for two seasons, and most women are happy to oblige. Both retail stores and clothing consignment shops thrive because of the inordinate need to discard and replace clothing too good to throw away. Repairing torn or worn clothing is a frugality of another century. When is the last time you noticed someone wearing darned socks or a patched jacket?

Cars offer another example of measuring our worth by constant consumption. Following World War II, the American dream was to have a car in every garage. I grew up in a nuclear family with two parents and three children. We had one family car. Fifty-some years later, the dream has expanded to a car for every driver in the family. My newspaper carrier, who actually lives in my neighborhood, has six brothers. For a few years, eight cars spilled out of his family's driveway and into the street. Likewise, for a short window of time, my husband, two sons, and I each left home every morning in our own automobile. We rationalized this arrangement as a necessity because of distance to work and conflicting schedules and the like. In truth, it was a convenience, not a necessity.

Popular leasing arrangements allow people to continuously drive new cars. Corporate job perks, which frequently include car allowances, also allow many people to biannually purchase or lease a new car. Pure desire to be behind the wheel of the latest model-year car with all its gimmicks and gadgets lures others into continually trading in last year's model. Thus, cars, one of America's most conspicuous status symbols, have also become disposable items. Newness of the car is of utmost importance. Preteens whine about having to ride in an older car if they're going to be picking up friends, and their friends comment on the quality and caliber of the car that will deliver them to whatever planned event is on the weekend roster. The youthful sensitivity to being taxied around in a "beater" obviously sprouts from catty adult comments. The sensitivity to driving an older car transfers easily to parents as they drive their children to the hockey arena and park their eight-year-old Toyota in a row of SUVs that look as if they just rolled off the carrier. The size of the vehicle is not directly related to the size of families today, but rather to the need for space to seat the children's teammates and friends who need to be driven to sports events or movies or wherever in style.

A shiny new truck in the driveway is usually a giveaway to a teenager in the house. High school parking lots are filled with trucks. My nephew, as a high school senior, proudly showed me his new green Ford pickup, which he fondly referred to as a "chick mobile." "It attracts the girls like a magnet," he told me. "They love to ride in trucks." Whether or not the truck is a magnet for girls, it certainly is highly prestigious for both boys and girls to have one to drive to school. In fact, I am not entirely convinced that the parents, who usually make the payments on these trucks, don't enjoy owning them equally as much as their children do. I've heard weak justifications for their purchase, such as trucks are really useful for hauling yard refuse or home-building supplies or the Christmas tree (all of which must have been hauled somehow in the pretruck days), as well as more convincing reasons related to trucks providing a greater degree of safety for their children in case of accidents. The point is this: A decade or so ago, most teens would have rather taken the notoriously inferior school bus to school than be seen driving a truck anywhere in the vicinity of a school parking lot. Today, the cool teen drives a truck, PT Cruiser, SUV, Jeep, or VW Bug. The era of being thrilled to drive to school in Grandma's like-new, twelve-year-old Buick, showing only 24,000 miles on the odometer, has disappeared.

Parents believe that they and their children are in some way better served by having the newest of what money can buy, including cars. Self-esteem and status have become regretfully intertwined. Status comes with driving a new car or truck to school and with parking several cars in the driveway at home; the trendier and newer the style, the better. If it's time to ratchet up the status and dispose of the old car, any number of charities will gladly take used cars, like Grandma's, that are in fine working condition. The charities will also happily provide you with a tax-deductible receipt for your gift.

Schools, now regarded as commodities, also have limited shelf lives. They, too, are disposable. In the span of thirty to forty years, school buildings become woefully outdated to the users. The facility that doesn't have a spacious media center, multiple indoor and outdoor areas for physical education, open space for gathering, a modern cafeteria, and a technology lab sporting brightly colored iMacs simply isn't up to par. The fact that the strength of a school should be measured by its instructional staff and working environment rather than its computer lab or media center doesn't always make a difference when parents come to an open house shopping for their child's school.

The budget ax is another mechanism to mothball outdated buildings. School districts that fail to pass a levy referendum often are forced to close a school to balance the budget. The oldest building usually is the first to close, regardless of the quality of the education provided by the school staff. Given the choice between enrolling in two equally superior schools, one housed in a new building and the other in an older, updated building, the new is the people's choice. If adults embrace this sort of rampant materialism, is it any wonder that children are susceptible to the same malady?

Materialistic American cultural values flourish in the classroom. Teachers are forced to compete with the marketplace and find this an impossible task. Their inability to do so, however, offers a healthy antidote for the overwhelming consumer culture that bombards schoolchildren. Classrooms should be comfortable educational settings, not showrooms; books and curricular materials should invite children to learn, not entertain them; teachers should be valued for the vital role they play in the learning process, not viewed as day-care providers and expected to be performers.

Preschool children often find their classroom toys and manipulatives boring and, in some cases, too well worn to even touch. The child-sized household appliances and rumpled costumes on the clothes rack in no way rival the playthings many children have at home. Too frequently, the learning activities don't measure up either. The local science museum, children's museum, or nature center offers far more stimulating activities than the classroom teacher ever could. By the time children exit the primary grades, their dissatisfaction with what the average classroom offers becomes even more apparent. "Cornucopia children,"[3] as they've been called, laden with too much of the best of everything, find school life quite dull.

One way teachers can combat clashing with the marketplace is to re-format the traditional curriculum to reduce materialism. For instance, many primary-grade teachers have abandoned the venerable classroom staple "show-and-tell" because of the unhealthy competition the activity generates between children and among parents. Other teachers have kept the concept but have changed the rules so that children can bring only specific types of items, such as those that are handmade or natural, to show to their classmates.

Additionally, some teachers no longer purchase any classroom decorations and manipulatives that are mass-produced.[4] Commercially crafted bulletin-board borders and holographic alphabet letters have been replaced by student artistry. Student work has replaced Hallmark posters in classrooms. Students in the elementary teacher education program at the university where I work learn to make their own manipulatives in science and math methods classes. Dyed pasta in a variety of shapes and bottle caps from different types of soda delight children as counting devices. Students planning to teach English, social studies, and science classes work feverishly at designing new units of study that explore advertising, economics, ecology, and other issues related to consumer consumption. Physically reducing consumerism in the classroom through recycling and careful consumption of goods also teaches students to prioritize the need for excessive buying and acquisition.

In some classrooms, teachers ask parents not to send toys with their children for recess play because toys limit the opportunity children have to be imaginatively playful. Many parents encourage children to stage TV and movie reproductions under the guise of creativity. Unfortunately, these children begin to confuse their images with TV and movie images and simple reproduction with creative imagination.[5] Similarly, preteens and teens confuse reality TV with life. Eventually, children become disinterested in imagining any world beyond what they have experienced on the screen. Introducing imagination into the curriculum sends teachers scurrying to seek staff development activities and workshops related to using the imagination and simple, generic manipulatives as both teaching and learning tools. Helping children interact with ordinary items used for daily living, rather than with commercially packaged toys and games, is another way teachers can reduce materialism in the classroom.

The back-to-school fashion sales that target students and parents each autumn present one of the most daunting commercial forces with which middle school and high school teachers and administrators must contend. While parents agree that their children should be appropriately dressed for school, some argue that schools have no right to determine what their kids should wear to class. Parents, formerly the fashion police, no longer make the rules governing the best dressed list. Students want to wear what they see modeled on television, pictured in teen fashion magazines, and displayed in retail stores like the Gap, American Eagle, and Abercrombie & Fitch.

The disturbing glitch is that marketers are in business to capture the gold, not to differentiate between tasteful and trashy clothes. What fashion moguls hail as the hottest look is clearly not what educators and parents always find acceptable. Most schools forbid gang-related apparel, attire that advertises drugs or alcohol, shirts that boast obscene or discriminatory slogans, and sexually provocative clothes. Nonetheless, teachers and administrators struggle with how to respond to bare midriffs, bejeweled belly buttons, low-cut tank tops, underwear hanging out of shorts and jeans, and ultra-low-rise blue jeans. It goes without saying that provocation is in the eye of the beholder.

Visiting a local high school, I noticed so many girls wearing low-rise blue jeans and their accompanying bare stomachs that I asked a group of them if they had stock in the Gap. Amid the giggles, one girl told me that they actually had a rule about not showing their stomachs, but they got away with wearing cropped tops and low-cut jeans by pulling their tops down around certain teachers. A few girls said they kept a sweater in their lockers, just in case. My assumption is that each girl left home wearing the sweater, which was immediately stuffed in the locker at school. One generously sized girl announced that she had never been sent home or told to cover up because nobody bothered to look at her.

School uniforms scream out as a simplistic answer to a situation that has gotten completely out of control. Staff members and parents with children in public schools that have chosen to adopt a school uniform applaud the choice. Not only is the uniform a status leveler among students, it also serves to dry up a relatively subjective disciplinary arena. However, it has taken advertisers years to groom the adolescent sales market. In 1997, ten-to nineteen-year-olds spent \$91.5 billion on consumable goods.[6] Merchandisers are not about to let this lucrative field dry up.

James Farrell writes:

> Americans learn to shop almost from birth. The average American child makes a first trip to a mall at two months of age. By two years, this average kid can name a product. By four, they can evaluate a product, and at six they've internalized the idea that "better brands cost more." At the relatively late age of eleven, they begin to understand that some claims are misleading. By adulthood, the average American of the Nineties consumes twice as many goods and services as the average American of 1950, and ten times as much as a counterpart from 1928.[7]

These facts give credence to the success of advertisers in creating a marketplace culture of materialism in the United States of America.

A report prepared by The Harwood Group[8] to examine patterns of consumption in the United States from the perspective of its own citizens asked people in Dallas, Los Angeles, Indianapolis, and Frederick, Maryland, to describe their beliefs about the role of consumption in society. The report outlines four findings:

1. Americans believe our priorities are out of whack. People of all backgrounds share certain fundamental concerns about the values they see driving our society. They believe materialism, greed, and selfishness increasingly dominate American life, crowding out a more meaningful set of values centered on family, responsibility, and community. People express a strong desire for a greater sense of balance in their lives—not to repudiate material gain, but to bring it more into proportion with the nonmaterial rewards of life.

2. Americans are alarmed about the future. People feel that the material side of the American Dream is spinning out of control, that the effort to keep up with the Joneses is increasingly unhealthy and destructive: 'The Joneses is killing me,' declared a man in one focus group. People are particularly concerned about the implication of our skewed priorities for children and future generations—they see worse trouble ahead if we fail to change course.

3. Americans are ambivalent about what to do. Most people express strong ambivalence about making changes in their own lives and in

our society. They want to have financial security and live in material comfort, but their deepest aspirations are nonmaterial ones. People also struggle to reconcile their condemnation of other Americans' choices on consumption with their core belief in the freedom to live as we choose. Thus, while people may want to act on their concerns, they are paralyzed by the tensions and contradictions embedded in their own beliefs. In turn, they shy away from examining too closely not only their own behavior, but that of others.

4. Americans see the environment as connected to these concerns—in general terms. People perceive a connection between the amount we buy and consume and their concerns about environmental damage, but their understanding of the link is somewhat vague and general. People have not thought deeply about the ecological implications of their own lifestyles; yet there is an intuitive sense that our propensity for "more, more, more" is unsustainable.[9]

Obviously, the problems cited in the Harwood report criticize our materialistic society. Most people would agree that our pervasive materialism contributes to a host of other problems facing the United States. Few of us could deny that we buy things we don't really need. An overriding concern for all of us should be that our mania for more of everything is unsustainable. The bright side to this depressing pattern of overconsumption, however, is the recognition of this complex social problem by economists, policymakers, educators, and the general public. We realize, as the Harwood report states, that in our ambivalence to changing our habits of overconsumption, we find ourselves part of "a society at odds with our values."[10]

Convincing the advertising world that we won't respond to its degrading marketing messages or that we will no longer be pressured into buying what we don't really want or need represents a serious, long-term challenge. A late-summer mailing I received from a national catalog retailer boldly stated, "The best dressed kids have the smartest parents." Literally no thinking person could believe this to be true, including the ad's copywriter. Nonetheless, this thoughtless piece of advertising was delivered to hundreds of thousands of households as an incentive to buy back-to-school clothes.

Historically, when society has found itself at odds with a perplexing social dilemma, it has looked to the school systems for help. Creating curricula that teach students to become wary consumers and good stewards of the land should be a welcome challenge to educators, one that some teachers have already taken on. Reducing materialism in the classroom is another step teachers should readily embrace. Teachers know how to simplify. Their value to society has never resulted in salaries that can maintain excessive consumption. I believe they are ready and waiting to model responsible consumerism in the classroom. When parents join hands with teachers to support the effort to free children from the unhealthy, competitive forces of the marketplace, destructive materialism will lose its appeal.

NOTES

1. "Consumer Culture: Spending Trends," *Faces of the New Millennium,* at pubweb.nwu.edu/~eyc345/finalspending.html, 1999 (accessed December 28, 2001).

2. David Walsh, *Selling Out America's Children* (Minneapolis, Minn.: Fairview, 1995).

3. *Cornucopia children* is a term B. A. Baldwin uses to describe wealthy children "who grow up with expectations (based on years of experience in the home) that the good life will always be available for the asking whether they develop personal accountability and achievement or not" (Baldwin, "The Cornucopia Kids," *US Air Magazine,* no. 10 [November 1989]: 30–34, quote on 31).

4. Carol Benson Holst, "Buying More Can Give Children Less," *Young Children,* vol. 54, no. 5 (September 1999): 19–23.

5. Holst, "Buying More Can Give Children Less."

6. "Consumer Culture," *Faces of the New Millennium.*

7. James Farrell, "Shopping: The Moral Ecology of Consumption," at www.stolaf.edu/people/farrellj/COURSES/Shopping-AS.html, 1998 (accessed October 1, 2001).

8. The Harwood Group, "Yearning for Balance: Views of Americans on Consumption, Materialism, and the Environment," *Sustainable Consumption & Production Linkages Virtual Policy Dialog,* at www.iisd.ca/linkages/consume/harwood.html, 1995 (accessed October 3, 2001).

9. The Harwood Group, "Yearning for Balance."

10. The Harwood Group, "Yearning for Balance."

5

A Landscape of Fear

The challenges of change are always hard. It is important that we begin to unpack those challenges that confront this nation and realize that we each have a role that requires *us* to change and become more responsible for shaping our own future.

—Hillary Rodham Clinton

"Who's afraid of the big bad wolf, the big bad wolf, the big bad wolf? . . . " You are; I am; we all are. As the present-day "wolf" morphs into the fear of failure, the specter of loneliness, the fear of violence, the pressure of commitment, and other typical fears, the greatest fear should be whether or not America will recognize the wolf. The "tra-la-la" behavior evidenced in the children's tale of "The Three Little Pigs" should cause us to reflect on how we live together in the world and how we are teaching our children to learn to do likewise.

Morning after morning, young children march off to wait for the school bus fearing the bullies on the corner, dreading peer rejection, and apprehensive about academic failure. Teenagers head into their respective school buildings dragging similar anxieties with them—anxieties reinforced by entryway metal detectors and key cards for admission. Inside their school buildings, they're greeted with prominently placed placards touting zero-tolerance policies and phone numbers posted for anonymous tips. Some students chat with police patrolling the premises before they make their way to their classrooms; a few nervously giggle about the morning's panic drill to prepare them for the possibility of a violent, life-threatening school eruption. Few, if any, question the legacy of Columbine.[1]

The hidden curriculum that dictates the informal learning in schools includes a new social agenda for finessing tranquillity. Teachers readily agree that fear inhibits learning and teaching, but they aren't necessarily in agreement about whose responsibility it is to deal with peacekeeping in the schools. Nevertheless, they now add a "fear-fighter" hat to those they already wear.

Rough-and-tumble America is becoming a fear-filled country. Citizens pay dearly for products and devices that provide an aura of safety and security. The tasteful front-yard sign that warns away intruders along with the monthly bill for the system that connects you to the community's essential safety services buy peace of mind, especially if you don't know your neighbors. Privacy fences keep neighborhood outsiders out and insiders securely in their private world. Cell phones, allowing for a 24-7 swirl of business, family, and social life, entice addicted users into believing they're in control of their lives. Besides offering instantaneous communication, they also offer constant companionship. No self-respecting high school student would be without one. Air-purification systems, with inviting names like Ionic Breeze, kill airborne bacteria with ultraviolet germicidal protection, and personal air purifiers for frequent travelers even fool wearers into believing that their personal air-space in the packed-to-the-gills 747 will be rarefied. Bottled waters travel with us like adult pacifiers in purses, briefcases, and backpacks and guarantee us not only a calorie-free drink, but also a purified one, whenever the need arises. Although entrepreneurs have become wealthy by designing products that are supposed to dilute our fears, the products do nothing to promote respectful, human relationships that encourage understanding and acceptance of others. They mask the basic unspoken fear that confronts humanity, which is all about how we might harmoniously live together in our ever-compacting world.

Parents, charged with the responsibility of laying the initial psychological building blocks that enable their children to feel safe and secure, are eager to look to others for help. They rely on teachers and caregivers to help them to teach preschool children to look both ways before crossing the street, not to speak to strangers, and so forth. Television's perenially popular Mr. Rogers[2] helped guide generations of children through the everyday difficulties and anxious moments of childhood, and *Sesame Street, Barney & Friends,* and other TV programs and videotapes for children continue to do the same. Primary school teachers try to ease children's fears by turning to children's literature for discussions about whom to trust, and police officers, firefighters, and medical personnel also join in educating children about safety and health issues through a variety of community programs. Even so, teachers, parents, and students no longer consider neighborhoods and schools naturally safe havens. Bullying, teasing, and harassment now constitute a way of life for children in and out of school.

Bullying behavior is not a recent phenomenon. Literature is rife with tales of youthful protagonists confronting bullies, from Charles Dickens's Oliver Twist[3] and David Copperfield[4] to Mark Twain's Tom Sawyer[5] to the contemporary and invincible Harry Potter,[6] a literary hero of the middle school set. Harry Potter's fear of bullies is like every child's fear, but in convincing readers and viewers that good will triumph over evil, Harry provides children with a glimmer of hope that is absent for too many of today's children.

During my childhood, adults summarily dismissed youthful bullies as neighborhood menaces. Neighborhood children knew who the bullies were and tried to sidestep them; parents and teachers knew who the bullies were and did their best to keep tabs on their behavior. This was a simple solution for a time that no longer exists, and it usually worked. One memorable occasion when I found myself caught in a power game of intimidation and fear remains remarkably clear to me, a testimony to the long-term impact of being the recipient of bullying behavior.

I was an avid ice-skater. The year I turned eleven years old, my closest friends cautioned me to stay clear of the skating rink because a twelve-year-old girl, named Barbara, was "out to get me." In the neighborhood mythology, Barbara "ruled" the outdoor rink. I was confident that I could easily outskate her, so I disregarded my girlfriends' warnings. Besides that, my parents had given me a wonderful pair of new skates for Christmas that year, and I loved the feeling of flying like the wind with them.

One afternoon, my friends saw Barbara slink into the warming house at the recreation center and slip a note into my boots. The note, a sort of a preteen Mafia message, warned me to never even consider coming to the skating rink again. Disregarding the warning as ridiculous, I continued to go to the neighborhood rink to skate every day after school as usual.

Within a week or so, Barbara started to aggressively harass me in person. Whenever she saw me in school or walking in the neighborhood, she would make gestures in the air with her hands like a professional boxer. If I was within hearing range, she would mutter under her breath about how she would rearrange my face if she ever saw me at the skating rink again. For days, I walked to school in fear of meeting up with Barbara, the terror of the seventh grade.

One Saturday, she caught me off guard. She cornered me in the girls' rest room in the recreational center and boxed my face in front of what seemed like the entire preteen world. I was humiliated and terrified. I immediately told my parents the sordid little story. They dismissed Barbara as a foolish neighborhood girl who liked to "talk big" and had deplorably bad manners. They suggested I just ignore her (which, in my naivete, I had been studiously doing) and didn't seem to recognize my fear.

The next time I went skating, Barbara was again lying in wait for me. She grabbed my skates and ran away with them as I was taking my boots off to lace up. She bolted out the door of the recreation center, shrieking with laughter and taunting me to come get my skates. I went home in tears and fearfully made up excuses for days about having too much homework to go skating.

For a week, Barbara teased me in school to come get my skates. Fearing my parents' response to my lost skates as much as I feared Barbara's tormenting behavior, I finally decided that telling my parents the truth about my skates was the lesser torment. I painfully recounted the whole story to my mother and then later to my father. Recognizing my anguish and fear this time, they tried to reassure me that everything would work out. The next morning at breakfast, my dad handed me my skates. "Take good care of these," he said. And almost as an afterthought, he added, "Don't worry about Barbara. She won't give you any more trouble."

I narrate this story to demonstrate a dramatic change in American culture. Bullying, once considered a neighborhood or schoolyard affair that seldom caused long-term anxiety, has become a national concern. My parents were able to deftly handle my ice-skating trauma, which they perceived as less than alarming and, in fact, typical kids' stuff. However, I grew up in a two-parent household in which getting along with others (including my own siblings) was an expectation. My parents wouldn't have dreamed of involving my teachers in this situation. First I was chided for waiting a week before I told my mother and father the truth about my sudden disinterest in skating. Then they decided how they would confront the issue. For them, the decision was easy. They knew, in a community sense, who Barbara was and who her parents were. Both families had children in the same school, attended the same church, and shopped at the same grocery store. People who lived in the same community needed to get along with one another. It was a simple maxim. My father drove over to Barbara's house and spoke to Barbara and her parents face-to-face.

I was thrilled and mortified at the same time when my father handed me my skates; but, most importantly, I was secure in believing I wouldn't have to worry about Barbara's harassment anymore. I never found out how Barbara's parents reacted to my father's visit, but I do know her mother was true to her word when she told my father that Barbara would never bother me again. Indeed, Barbara never so much as glanced in my direction again.

Today, the stakes for students, parents, and teachers are significantly higher. Neighborhood schools are all but passe, so parents of schoolchildren no longer have even a nodding acquaintance with one another. There isn't a sense of acceptable community behavior, because neighborhood communities, where they still exist, have given way to a neighborhood minus the community aspect. The school has become the common factor in bringing people together, but community in most schools is little more than advertising rhetoric. Bullies in schools, more dangerous and sophisticated in their approaches to terrorizing classmates, command nationwide attention and fear.

TV shows like *NYPD Blue* and *Law and Order,* depicting glamorized episodes of violent struggles between good and evil, pale in the face of live reporters playing footage of school cafeterias where teenage students shot and killed their classmates. The images of Dylan Klebold and Eric Harris, the high school executioners at Columbine High School in Colorado, remain etched in the minds of students, teachers, and parents. Peer victims, stretched to the breaking point by bullying classmates, have forced the public to respond seriously to bullying behavior and threats of violence in schools and forced teachers and administrators to scramble to enact strategic plans to deal with school violence.

The American Association of University Women reports that four out of five students in grades 8–11 personally experience harassment in school, with girls experiencing more harassment than boys by only a slight margin.[7] Xin Ma[8] examined the cycle of bullying in grades 6–8 and found that a disciplined school climate helps victims of bullying and discourages bullying itself. In "Getting to the Heart of Safety," Margaret M. Sagarese and Charlene C. Gianetti[9] discuss the atmosphere of cruelty that pervades schools today and indicate that mean-spiritedness paves the way for a climate of humiliation and intimidation that undermines any school's overt curriculum. These reports and others underline the dramatic need for students, parents, and teachers to combat the draining effect that fear has on children.

Fear of being hurt, bullied, or harassed in school obviously causes a climate of distrust. It also destroys students' and teachers' freedom in the classroom. Put-downs and hurtful slurs that children learn from movies, sitcoms, shock jocks, CDs, families, and friends too frequently find their way into classroom discussion. Degrading comments paralyze eager students into silence. A quiet "book nerd" is often a bully's favorite target. Teachers regretfully find that bullying and teasing also create negative repercussions for small-group work. Avoidance behavior surfaces when students, and sometimes parents, insist on specific seating arrangements in an effort to control or avoid constant harassment from certain children. Teachers, already careful to group students of differing abilities for cooperative work, have yet another variable to consider. When policing the classroom takes precedence over teaching and learning, it becomes more prudent to assign students a chapter to read than to risk creating an opportunity for dialogue that might put some students in jeopardy.

Attendance patterns change for students who face daily harassment, grades decline, and simmering hurt can turn to vengeful rage. When truancy feels safer than the classroom, when failure feels safer than academic success, and when striking back becomes the ultimate answer to school oppression, work sheets won't mend the situation.

The cataclysmic events of September 11, 2001, that rocked America's sensibility have added a nerve-wracking and unanticipated layer of anxiety to our culture. The devastation of the attacks on the World Trade Center and the Pentagon, the crash of Flight 93, and the subsequent war on terrorism indelibly etched new fears into the hearts of everyone living in the United States. Freedom and democracy, constructs taken for granted and perhaps thoughtlessly internalized, constitute American identity. Violently stripped of our identity by these unanticipated attacks, we found ourselves face-to-face with fear of terrorists and with restricted freedoms—new enemies that we are ill prepared to handle politically, economically, and psychologically. The emotional numbness following September 11 forced teachers to design lessons to help students confront additional fears at the same time they were trying to understand and reconcile their own.

The twenty-two adult students I met with three days after the terrorist attacks faced me with incomparable intensity. The need to process the situation took precedence over the assigned subject matter. We discussed fear and dread of war and mourned the needless loss of lives. We debated the effects of imperialism and tried to connect the dots to explain terrorist behavior. We searched for life's meaning in a culture of extremists who crave death for a cause.

What primarily captured my attention, however, was the staggering sense of this event as a whole as a cultural reference point that signaled the need for a change in Americans' life patterns. The fear expressed by these adult students was overwhelmingly real, but it spoke to deeper issues than September 11 itself. The underlying fear they uncovered was the discomforting sense of naivete we display with regard to freedom. We glibly hoist up freedom as the American way of life because we come and go as we please, we work and play where we choose, we say whatever pops out of our mouths, we read anything in print, and we openly challenge our leaders. The problem accompanying this taken-for-granted attitude is that it has become so pervasive that we no longer are able to critically assess our condition of freedom. We don't look beyond or beneath the sensationalized news in print or on film that we accept as gospel. We denounce terrorism without understanding what it means or why the United States became a target, just as we minimize violence in schools without exploring the sociocultural factors that lead to the incidents.

A first-grade teacher told me about her students' reactions to the crisis events. As expected, the first graders evidenced a variable range of understanding of the actual events, but she was struck by their sense of what she termed "intangible fear." She had to dry the tears of a child who came to school distraught because his mother, who traveled frequently for her job, had gone to the airport that morning to fly to another city. This seemed to be an understandable fear, but as she tried to comfort this little tyke, she realized it wasn't the fear of another terrorist event or hijacked plane that was upsetting him. His mother had explained all that she needed to about that situation to him. This bright little boy was crying because "nothing seems right; everybody looks sad." He wanted his mother home so she could help him take the nation's pulse. "Children read our faces in school," this teacher said. "When we are tense, the children react accordingly. Since September 11, they worry that we know something we aren't sharing. They're frightened and confused about what they should fear, and so are we."

The first grader and the adult students expressed similar anxiousness in separate contexts regarding the evolution of some unidentified fear in our culture following September 11. Both the child and the adults simplistically wanted to believe good things happen to good people; and, seemingly, Americans are good people. When we find an event to be tragically incomprehensible, we begin to look for someone or something to blame. Finding a scapegoat temporarily eases the tragedy. We wanted to determine causality in the terrorist attacks, so we could find and punish the evildoers. Then we could put the situation to bed and get on with our lives. But we haven't been able to affix blame. Multiple questions, possibilities, hints, and suggestions have created a confusing array of ideas governing right and wrong. The public has been left with an unsettling sense of fear.

School bullying offers a parallel scene. News reports profile the typical case like this: A group of tenth-grade boys tease and bully Paul; he is stunned, hurt, and feels victimized. He hasn't done anything to warrant this treatment except to get straight A's. He becomes increasingly more withdrawn in class and talks to almost no one in school. He shares his fear with his best friend, who tells him that their classmate Todd is the ringleader. Paul finally confides to his father that he is being constantly bullied and is considering dropping out of school, but his father insists this is nonsense. He tells Paul to ignore the bullying and mind his own business.

Eventually, Paul can't take any more teasing. He believes nobody cares about his torment. In desperation, he decides to talk to a teacher he admires about Todd. Paul trusts the teacher when he says he'll talk to Todd about his behavior. When the bullying and teasing continue, Paul becomes depressed. He doesn't trust anyone. He blames everybody for his living hell, including his parents, his teachers, and his classmates. He decides to show his peers what it's like to be bullied. He brings a rifle to school one day and mentally snaps. Reporters race to the site to film the carnage for the evening news. School is never the same for those students and teachers. Who should shoulder the blame?

Fear of school violence can't be adequately addressed by a simple case profile or with pat solutions. It is one variable of a complex societal issue that both creates and sustains the problem. However, teachers can address the culture that creates comfortable conditions for school violence within their classrooms. They can also tenaciously hang on to their freedom to teach. Teachers must be alert to their surroundings. They need to be a humanized rendition of a home security system. Metaphorically, if a student pushes the wrong buttons in the classroom, a warning signal should buzz for the teacher. Disruptive behavior is predictable behavior for alert teachers. Vigilance diffuses much inappropriate behavior. Zero tolerance doesn't apply only to weapons.

Teaching means leading. Responsible leadership mandates that teachers lead the students and not vice versa. A responsible leader models respect and expects it of followers. Teachers and students, as members of a learning community, should be held to mutually agreeable classroom guidelines. Insensitive behavior toward other students doesn't belong in any classroom. A classroom community should publicly decide on and post community behavior rules that include, at the very least, a reminder that everyone has an equal right to live peacefully on this earth, a mandate to respect all people, a call for academic honesty, and zero tolerance for student put-downs.

Maxine Greene tells us that "children who have been provoked to reach beyond themselves, to wonder, to imagine, to pose their own questions are the ones most likely to learn to learn."[10] Teachers, as provocateurs, believe that nothing trivial occurs in a learning situation. They won't miss the opportunity to intervene as often as necessary to maintain a comfortable learning environment that embraces freedom of expression, freedom to learn, and freedom from fear. They will steadfastly refuse to become victims of fear who give up their right to teach. This is the foremost prospect for carrying on the discussion that will teach children to continually question how we might fearlessly live together on this planet.

NOTES

1. Columbine is the name of the high school in Littleton, Colorado, that was the scene of the gory mass killing of classmates and teachers on April 20, 1999, committed by Eric Harris and Dylan Klebold.

2. Mr. Fred Rogers, an ordained minister, was the host of the immensely popular children's television show *Mister Rogers' Neighborhood* for thirty-three years.

3. Charles Dickens, *Oliver Twist* (London: Octopus Books, 1981).

4. Charles Dickens, *David Copperfield* (New York: Penguin, 1997).

5. Mark Twain, *The Adventures of Tom Sawyer* (New York: Viking, 1987).

6. J. K. Rowling, *Harry Potter and the Sorcerer's Stone* (New York: Scholastic, 1997).

7. Harris Interactive, *Hostile Hallways: Bullying and Teasing* (Des Moines, Iowa: Newton Manufacturing, 2001).

8. Xin Ma, "Bullying and Being Bullied: To What Extent Are Bullies Also Victims?" *American Education Research Journal,* vol. 38, no. 2 (Summer 2001): 351–370.

9. Margaret M. Sagarese and Charlene C. Gianetti, "Getting to the Heart of Safety," *Schools-in-the-Middle,* vol. 9, no. 1 (September 1999): 7–10.

10. Maxine Greene, *The Dialectic of Freedom* (New York: Teachers College Press, 1988), 14.

6

From Aesop to ASAP

There is more to life than increasing its speed.

—Mohandas Gandhi

You won't find *Aesop's Fables*[1] making the middle school "Top Ten Cool Books" reading list. My bellwether fifth graders helped me to understand why the Greek fabulist's tales are no longer cool. During a classroom visit, I discussed storytelling with them as both a narrative art for communicating and a method for learning that preceded reading and writing. The middle school group understood that idea perfectly and cavalierly voted to warp backward in time to learn without having any written homework. They gave a thumbs-down to *Aesop's Fables,* however, because the stories therein were "stupid," in their words. Not one of the twenty-four bright, young faces thought that the "Tortoise and the Hare"[2] made any sense at all. The embedded moral, "Slow but steady wins the race," didn't pop out to them as one of life's lessons to embrace. (In truth, most of them weren't up to formulating the "moral" as Aesop intended anyway.)

The eleven-year-olds insisted that the tortoise would really be the loser today because, again in their words, "being slow never gets you anywhere." They used car racing as an analogy. If the fastest car in a race breaks down, the mechanics fix it immediately and the driver still has a chance to win because, overall, the driver has an edge. In any event, there isn't a chance that the slowest, last-place car will end up winning the race. They decided that if they rewrote the fable, the hare would win by a mile.

He would train for the race, of course, and be in peak condition so there would be no need for him to lie down. The moral of their new-age fable would be "Fast and conditioned wins the race." And so the ancient Aesop gives way to the trendy ASAP.

I shouldn't have been surprised at the fifth graders' attempt to update Aesop. After all, this is the "instant breakfast" generation. Their parents jet across the country for business meetings, and their grandparents grocery shop via SimonDelivers.com. One of the first lessons they learned in school was to manage the limited amount of time they had each day in which to learn their lessons, complete their work, eat their lunch, and play their games at recess. Given society's edification of speed, the adage "Slow but steady wins the race" is easy to ignore.

Aesop and the Greeks paid homage to Hermes,[3] the swift messenger to the deities, and the ancient Romans revered the fleet-winged Mercury,[4] who served in the same capacity to their gods. Postmodern Americans reify Immediacy in the form of online instant messaging services, express delivery, instant credit, urgent care, and instant replays.

By honoring all that is immediate, American society has allowed the whole concept of *ASAP* to define who we are and how we behave. Consider drivers, for instance, who assume a behind-the-wheel persona that shows a distinct reverence for speed and a disregard for safety. There are those drivers who routinely ignore posted speed limits, those who refuse to merge in an orderly fashion at a flashing warning sign and inconsiderately race to the head of the traffic line, and those who weave like chess players muscling their cars into the merging traffic. Harried grocery shoppers act much the same as they careen from one checkout lane to the next, heedless of whose heels they clip. They boldly assess the size of the order of the next person in line because they don't have time to wait their turn. Even social gatherings have taken on an air of urgency. People introduce themselves to strangers in intense, rapid-fire conversation by noting their personal accomplishments. They constantly keep a look out so as not to miss a networking possibility, then grab an hors d'oeuvre on the way out the door, allowing themselves just enough time to catch the final inning of their son's or daughter's Little League game. The manic pace of the Road Runner, exaggeratedly depicted as a Looney Tunes cartoon character in constant trouble because his only attribute is speed,[5] now serves as the benchmark for the standard pace of life. ASAP, god of the immediate, gave birth to an urgent lifestyle that causes us to revere quick accomplishment and ignore reflective practice.

Is it any wonder Aesop's tale of a tediously plodding tortoise means nothing to today's children? Fast-forward rules the domain. Preschoolers understand the FF technological command before they are developmentally able to conceptualize the subtleties of fast-forward behavior in their daily lives. However, by the time they begin school, they expect school life to flow speedily, if not merrily. Five-year-olds begin school eager to learn to read and write, but when the process is less than instantaneous, the result is often devastating for both students and parents. Children, raised to expect immediate action in an image-driven, technological society, quickly lose interest in spending a year's time or more to master the skills necessary for learning to read. Grade-schoolers complain that it takes too long to read an entire book, and, furthermore, it's boring.

Children and their adult mentors find it much quicker and eminently more stimulating to unravel a story visually with sound and color and action on the screen than to breathe life into the dull pages of manuscript print. Because children grow up in "cyberhood,"[6] the screen world of televisions, videos, computers, electronic games, the Internet, and MTV, they expect to learn everything quickly and in small doses. Reading a text as a way to gather information is in danger of becoming extinct for students who started learning in infancy from images and sound bites. Written assignments have become chores that students find tiresome and meaningless. Internet-generation parents tend to agree with their children. They believe their children learn more (and more quickly) from surfing the web, playing on a sports team, attending after-school sessions at for-profit institutions, and traveling across the country than they do from lengthy hours of book work. Some high schools no longer mandate homework for this very reason. Frustrated students, busy with after-school jobs or extracurricular activities that pique both their interests and their social lives, were choosing to ignore trivial pen-and-paper assignments with their parents' support. Battle-fatigued teachers at these schools eventually gave up chasing after late assignments, and traditional homework ended in these classrooms without so much as a whimper.

Meanwhile, as the debate ensues about what knowledge is worth learning and in what context, skillful, "reflective practitioners"[7] in the classroom struggle to update their pedagogy. These skillful teachers know that traditional models for delivering education won't take students where they need to go to thrive in the future. They also know that nothing will be gained by updating either curricula or instruction without teaching students how to think through the why and how of everything they learn. As they strive to incorporate the latest technology into the curriculum to stay abreast of their cyber-savvy students and to try to keep them interested in learning, they realize that technology is not the panacea to educational reform. They know there are no shortcuts to the learning process.

Nevertheless, each semester, I teach K–12 teachers who, while complaining about feeling compelled to shortcut the learning process to keep pace with the mandated curriculum, fall victim to their own complaints. These teachers are studying to become lead teachers and school administrators, and they try to rush pell-mell through a postgraduate degree by meeting the program requirements in the shortest amount of time possible. They are neither indolent nor indifferent to learning, but rather driven by school district policies that urge them to complete their degrees as quickly as possible so they can move forward in their careers.

Balancing their need for immediacy and their desire for scholarship presents me with an ongoing dilemma that I constantly weigh as a teacher. Adult students juggle their own education with careers and families and social obligations. They want to receive their class syllabus online before the class begins so they can plan on how to best economize on their time. They expect their work to challenge them, yet they want an instant blend of practicality and theory. They come to class bone tired at night and on weekends, and binge on their education, by cramming forty-five hours of class time into three Wednesday-Saturday-Wednesday sessions, for example, with a week's break in between each sequence. This means that Wednesday-night classes meet for three and one-half hours and that Saturday classes meet for eight hours. I tell these students I understand that they are giving up something to earn their degree, even though I know each one of them tries to juggle more than is possible and routinely cuts corners on studies.

Elementary teachers laugh and say they tell their students the same thing when they come to school tired from dance lessons and Tae Kwon Do. Secondary teachers nod in agreement and say their students hear the same thing from them when they come to class aching from football practice, exhausted from weekend social life, or sleepy from working too late.

The point is this: The pervasive pattern depicts an indigenous characteristic of American culture that we embrace. The cliché of living in the fast lane is a reality. Parents teach children how to maneuver schedules, become overinvested in too many activities, and prize speed above all else. K–12 teachers reinforce the same message daily for their students, and college professors demonstrate how to do this for teachers trying to earn advanced degrees.

When I tell adult students they have to give up something to gain something else, I need to make it worthwhile for them to give up watching television for a semester. If they choose to pare their volunteer coaching down to one team for the soccer season, they shouldn't have to regret their decision because my class wasn't worth it. This means that I need to figure out engaging, alternative pedagogical methods to teach these overbooked students for eight hours at a crack. While I need to constantly seek out new tools for my own toolbox, I also need to make sure I don't sacrifice student learning for "edutainment."[8] I need to ask questions that spur students to stretch in new directions, to awaken them to new ideas, to broaden their familiar paths.

I haven't given up on homework yet, but I have revised my thinking about what constitutes a meaningful assignment versus a seductive assignment. A meaningful assignment, at any grade level, develops and expands student thinking and asks students to demonstrate new understandings by making application in a broader context. It takes "soak time" for students to reflect on new learning and robust and creative planning on both the teachers' and students' part to demonstrate it. A seductive assignment, on the other hand, lures students into expanding on someone else's learning in superficial ways and doesn't require them to demonstrate their learning. Multiple assignments that require minimal time and minimal thinking easily seduce students into equating completion with learning. Task completion can also falsely seduce teachers into thinking student learning has occurred because they have numbers to average. In the final outcome, students often spend more time on seductive assignments than they should, learning less than they could. Keeping in mind that time is of ultimate value to students, I need to plan carefully how I will spend my time teaching and how I will ask my students to spend their time learning.

The same pedagogical principles hold true for teaching in elementary and secondary schools. Students typically sit in class for seven hours a day, five days a week. They also come to class spent from overbooked lives. They resent time-wasting activities and enjoy discovering and collaborating on new ideas that lead to meaningful learning, just like their adult counterparts. All teachers at every grade level need to determine how to best meet the needs of students who want to rush through life like Aesop's hare. The daunting task for teachers is to coach their students into top "condition" so that, in the end, they will win the race because they have learned to be critical and reflective thinkers along the way.

One approach for teaching the postmodern learner is to use constructivist concepts for learning that allow students to link previous knowledge and new learning together in ways that individually make sense to them. This Deweyan-based methodology[9] has students asking questions as well as answering them as they explore the connections between what they already know informally and what they are currently studying. Knowledge becomes a variable, a human construction, dependent upon the context and the times. The following lesson illustrates this concretely by contrasting a traditional approach to a language arts lesson for middle school students that focuses on how to formulate a story with a constructivist approach.[10]

A traditional way to teach students how to design a story would be to dissect the construction of a well-known short story, such as O. Henry's classic "The Ransom of Red Chief."[11] Typically, this would entail asking students to read the short story and then directing them to fill in the blanks on an accompanying work sheet. The students would identify such organizational concepts as the introduction, core, and conclusion to the story. They might be asked to match main characters with their actions and to write a sentence or two about the main point of the story.

Using a constructivist approach to the same assignment, a teacher could show the Hallmark video of the story to the class. The students could orally reconstruct the plot and identify a beginning, middle, and end to the story. They could identify the main characters in a variety of ways—for example, with a written description introducing the main characters to their friends or by role-playing and introducing the fictional characters to their classmates. Students could collaboratively work in small groups on identifying the theme using guided questions; they could create a new story using the same theme or watch the movie *Ruthless People,*[12] based on the same theme, and compare the two; they could use the theme to create a poem. As a finale, they could read the story to compare the visual with the written construction. The constructivist approach to the lesson would require far more preparation and learning time than the traditional approach, but it would also meet with far greater student interest because it would concretely connect the concept of literary construction of a plot to a medium to which the students could relate.

Experienced, traditional teachers frequently bristle at constructivist methodology because it requires them to depart from the canned curriculum in the guidebooks to transmit knowledge and teach in a facilitative way. New teachers fear constructivist teaching because it is too time-consuming. They learn to honor speed as they move into their careers. They learn to operate within a school year divided into learning periods or quarters, and they work hard to figure out how to cover a specific amount of the curriculum within the specified time frame. They learn to pace daily lessons so that units of learning take no longer than the teaching guidebook indicates, and they proudly send home newsletters to parents that list the learning activities accomplished during the week.

Constructivist teaching requires planning and preparation time that teachers don't have built into their schedules. It also forces some teachers to question whether or not they actually understand the learning process themselves. Naysayers indicate that the tried-and-true methods that teachers have used for generations still are the best. In reality, they are hesitant to depart from the traditional and familiar practices of teaching with which they are comfortable. They blame the district curriculum for being too inclusive and say they just can't fit everything in, much as they wish they could. In reality, they are concerned about teaching students to pass the standardized tests.

Although few teachers would categorize learning as an instant activity, many still treat teaching as if it were. They buy into outdated teaching practices of asking students to read a chapter from a textbook, fill in the work-sheet blanks, and pass their papers forward because it's a quick way to check off a lesson. They replicate instant teaching packages that require minimal output from them and minimal input from students because they don't have time to design new lessons and they feel pushed and hurried into being accountable for more content each year.

Does constructivist teaching pull teachers out of the speed trap in which they enmesh themselves? No, it decidedly does not; however, it does affirm their commitment to educate. By teaching students to connect new knowledge to what they already know and what is meaningful to them, teachers create a framework in which students can learn. Constructivist teachers lead students to discover how to plan for their own learning and, eventually, how to be able to think through complex ideas reflectively and critically.

Educators should feel compelled to take on the role of provocateurs. To do that, every teacher must stand up and rebel against being forced to deliver superficial instruction that too often poses for good education because it encompasses the fast-forward attribute that fits the current cultural pace. Children deserve the freedom to learn, and teachers deserve the freedom to teach. Both processes take time and reflection. A guaranteed way to short-circuit education is to package curricula and instruction as if they were microwavable snacks for students to munch on when they need some quick energy.

NOTES

1. Aesop was a Greek fabulist of the sixth century B.C.

2. "The Tortoise and the Hare" is a well-known fable by Aesop that tells a tale of a race between a plodding tortoise and a flashy, quick hare, who is overconfident of his ability to win the race. Ultimately, the tortoise crosses the finish line first because the hare fell asleep while taking a rest. Thus, Aesop embeds the moral we have come to know as "Slow but steady wins the race."

3. Hermes, in Greek mythology, was the god of commerce, cunning, invention, and theft. He served as messenger to the gods and patron of travelers.

4. Mercury, in Roman mythology, was the god of travel, commerce, and thievery. He served as messenger and herald to the gods and was renowned for his speed.

5. In 1949, Warner Brothers introduced the cartoons featuring Wile E. Coyote and the Road Runner.

6. David Walsh, Kristin Parker, and Monica Walsh, *Dr. Dave's Cyberhood* (New York: Simon & Schuster, 2001).

7. Donald Schon, *The Reflective Practitioner* (New York: Basic, 1983).

8. Carol Tell, "The I-Generation—From Toddlers to Teenagers: A Conversation with Jane M. Healy," *Educational Leadership,* vol. 58, no. 2 (October 2000): 11.

9. John Dewey's laboratory schools built curricula around knowledge familiar to students dealing with information related to family and community.

10. Jeannie Oakes and Martin Lipton, *Teaching to Change the World* (Boston: McGraw-Hill College, 1999).

11. William Sydney Porter, using the pen name of O. Henry, wrote "The Ransom of Red Chief" in 1910.

12. *Ruthless People* is a 1986 film starring Bette Midler and Danny DeVito that was based on O. Henry's short story "The Ransom of Red Chief."

7

Attention Seekers

Fame is a bee.
It has a song—
It has a sting—
Ah, too, it has a wing.

—Emily Dickinson

The sound of champagne corks popping followed by the unmistakable fountain of fizz focused my attention. Peering down on the floor of the arena, I noticed beach balls silently bobbling back and forth between the aisles and rubbery strands of string confetti swooshing into the audience and onto the floor. I became so caught up in the palpable sense of festivity that I nearly missed my son march by wearing the mortarboard with the iridescent gecko pasted on the top. I was sitting high in the arena with throngs of other parents and relatives looking down on a few thousand graduates, all dressed exactly alike in blue caps and gowns, come marching into the stadium. The clever signs, symbols, and sayings on the graduation caps provided singular amusement to the audience and also marked specific graduates. Without some distinctive symbol, no one seated in the arena seats would have been able to pinpoint the graduate they came to honor. I suddenly understood the gecko as more than the motif for the campus rock band in which my son played. I have often thought about this particular institution's graduation protocol, more gleeful than most I have experienced, and how it clearly exemplifies not only the competitive culture of one specific university, but also the human need for social interaction and validation of worth.

The graduates wanted the attention of their friends and family, and rightfully so. They attended college to single themselves out in the first place. In a ceremony where you stand up with your colleagues by discipline and have your bachelor of arts degree in English or bachelor of science degree in electrical engineering conferred en masse, there is little opportunity for individual attention during the official ceremony. The painstakingly personalized mortarboard scheme, seriously frowned on by the university, brought individual attention to these students. This student artifice, enacted in various ways at college graduations across the country, is simply a ritualistic culmination of years of learning how to seek attention.

Competing for attention is rampant enough in American society to consider it a national sport. Toddlers, children, teens, and adults preoccupy themselves with seeking attention and being seen, from pirouetting in BabyGap rompers to tattooing front teeth to driving BMWs. It is a social phenomenon that fuels the ego of both the young and the not so young. The uniquely individualistic endeavor of pursuing attention, however, also serves to divide people into social classes and bestows power on the already powerful.[1] The rich and famous, for example, not only have social status because of their wealth and claim to fame, but they also have power because of the attention they are able to command or buy, as the case may be.

The celebrity culture, largely created and supported by the media, has laid the framework for a cult of attention seekers. Perspicacious press agents spend their days spawning celebrities and live well from their offspring. Hollywood film celebrities, TV personalities, popular musicians, and national sports figures all thrive on the doting attention of the public and pursue as much media print and TV time as possible. This is partially responsible for keeping them famous, or at least in the public eye, and fortune generally follows fame.

Forbes magazine compiles an annual "Celebrity 100" list and uses a formula that combines earning power and star power that factors in the numbers of press citations, mentions on television and radio, feature stories in magazines, and web hits to determine who makes the list. In order, the top ten for the 2002 list were: Britney Spears, Tiger Woods, Steven

Spielberg, Madonna, U2, *NSYNC, Mariah Carey, Oprah Winfrey, Michael Jordan, and Tom Hanks.[2]

The year's top celebrity, barely out of her teens, released three hit albums; starred in *Crossroads,* a film that achieved lackluster ratings; opened Nyla, a New York restaurant; and earned $39.2 million.[3] What this models to Britney admirers is that getting attention makes all the difference, no matter how you pursue it. The top celebrities on the list are rich and powerful figures who have replaced society's heroes and heroines of a bygone era.

Some on the *Forbes* 100 list have achieved their status because of talent, but even those celebrities have aggressive managers and agents who know how to buy the right kind of attention. Celebrities of this sort represent the "haves" in a world divided into "haves" and "have-nots," and their status and wealth bestows them with power. If Michael Jordan endorses a brand of sneakers, every budding athlete wants to run in the shoes Jordan says are the best. It's as if somehow wearing the shoes will improve their athletic ability. His very endorsement bequeaths status to the wanna-bes. The Britney look does the same thing for middle school–aged girls who hope to gain popularity by slinging their jeans on their hips and strutting like the star. Even though people who can't lay claim to notable status find the attention-seeking antics of certain celebrities revolting and the sheer amount of attention paid to them excessive, they continue to feed on the flavorful media tidbits as armchair voyeurs, if not blatant consumers. More importantly, however, with the demise of the American hero, celebrity status has become so overemphasized that people falsely believe that the prescribed way to garner pleasure, fame, riches, and power is to gain attention. Despite weak protests, American society has done its best to institutionalize an individualistic, attention-seeking culture.

Parents aid and abet their children into developing into first-class attention seekers in one of two ways: as unwitting, overly devoted parents or as intentional, opportunistic parents. Both stay-at-home and working parents can unwittingly entice toddlers into attention mongering by focusing every second of their available time on their children. Children, shortchanged by this sort of parenting, quickly turn into tiny despots in their own households. They learn to apply the manipulative skills, honed from endless hours of interaction with indulgent parents, to seeking

whatever they want, wherever and whenever. These children, once referred to with clicking tongues as "spoiled," have turned into spoilers.
They spoil relaxing dinners in quiet restaurants, stirring movies in inti-
mate theaters, solemn church services, and classrooms across the country by their unbefitting, attention-seeking behaviors.

Opportunistic parents, who pursue every advantage for their children,
lure them into the attention-seeking culture by overscheduling them into
multiple activities. This roster of activity supposedly keeps parent and
child bonded in action, but it also sets the stage for children learning to
seek attention through continual preparation for performances. This trend
has given rise to a proliferation of entrepreneurial dance and music stu-
dios that offer lessons for children as young as two years old and endless,
costly recitals for admiring parents, innumerable camps for almost every
activity but camping, and community organizations that sponsor sports
activities for children so young that they are incapable of understanding
the rules of the game they are playing.

"Stage mothers"[4] provide a classic example of parents intent on prim-
ing their children for competitive activities that will make them world famous, or at least secure an opportunity for them to appear on stage for
public appraisal and approval. Such mothers (or fathers) co-opt their children into spending endless hours rehearsing song lyrics and dance steps
for beauty pageants, theatrical or film auditions, ice follies, or whatever.
They teach their children every preening technique in the book to maxi-
mize their chances of capturing a trophy, winning attention, and eventually fame and fortune, but they rationalize away the psychological damage they do to their children, not the least of which is robbing them of
childhood. The sensationalized 1996 Colorado murder case of JonBenet
Ramsey, described as "a painted baby, a sexualized toddler beauty
queen,"[5] widely exposed the improbable chance such children have to experience childhood.

Organized youth sports activities provide another example of the insti-
tutionalization of attention seeking. While there is no reason to question
participation in Little League or youth athletics, there is reason to question if the benefits are alleged or actual. Parents supposedly enroll children in sports activities to learn teamwork, cooperation, healthy fitness
habits, and positive notions about competition. However, the benefits
seem negligible when weighed against children's depression over missed

scoring opportunities; coaches' tantrums at umpires' calls; and parents screaming from the sidelines at coaches' calls, at players' mistakes, and at other parents who place cooperation above competition.[6] How do you explain the case of the "hockey dad death" to children? How is it that a parent with three sons on a hockey team can become so enraged at some bodychecking that occurred during a scrimmage that he beat another hockey dad to death?[7] Opportunistic parents obsessed with seeing that their sons and daughters get the attention needed for high school athletic stardom that might lead to college athletic scholarships—and, in some exceptional cases, professional fame—take the joy out of the game and negate the benefits gained from participation for everyone. Misplaced adult anger in youth sports activities, so commonplace that it seems almost acceptable, begs the question of teaching children about teamwork.

The Y-ers, the generation born between 1977 and 1995, have challenged classroom teachers about teamwork in previously undiscovered ways. This generation arrived in the kindergarten classroom so well schooled in competitive, attention-seeking behaviors that teachers openly welcomed cooperative learning[8] as a pedagogy to teach children about teamwork and cooperation. The Generation-Y children, who have grown up with material affluence, an overabundance of consumer options, youth-oriented marketing, and competing with their friends to do more and buy more, value attention more than anything else in the classroom. The current primary school students, sometimes referred to as the "rising millennial generation," are also better at brand names than book titles and far more concerned about how they look than how they learn.[9]

On a school visit not long ago, I had to make a wide arc as I walked past the girls' rest room. I asked a seventh or eighth grader what the occasion was that was causing the buzz. She excitedly bubbled, "I'm not sure. I can't see the whole thing, but it's cool." I moved on down the hall imagining that the girls were admiring someone's new outfit. Thirty minutes later, retracing my path, I came upon the same situation in the same place with another group of girls. Curiosity got the better of me, so I asked the same question and this time got another cryptic answer: "I think it's a party." There seemed to be high interest about something, but partying so overtly in the middle of a school day didn't make sense to me. As I rounded the corner, I saw the principal, a former student of mine, heading down the hallway. She didn't appear to be in any hurry, so I doubted that she was on a mission to break up an unwarranted party. Her first words were to laughingly ask me if I made it through the "gaggle of girls." She then unlocked the mystery for me.

At the beginning of the school year, one of the teachers told the principal and staff an amusing story about how difficult it was to keep up with the activities of her own teenage daughters and how she learned to communicate with them. She tried leaving messages on their cell phones, but they didn't respond, and e-mail went unanswered. In desperation, she finally hit on the perfect solution for anything she really wanted them to know or do. She put Post-it notes on the bathroom mirror. With a collective "aha," the seventh- and eighth-grade teachers decided this simple solution might have merit for in-school communications. Since that time, any important information for the seventh- and eighth-grade students gets posted on the bathroom mirrors.

It has apparently worked communication miracles. Physical appearance is a huge issue for these young teens, who make more than the necessary number of trips to the bathroom each day. The Post-it notices act like hot tips to the first few who see them, and word spreads like wildfire. The principal said, "We've learned to be clever, so the notices have the breezy tone of a casual note instead of a legitimate school memo. Communication is what we're after, and we usually follow up with an actual memo anyway. We still find the real memos in the wastebasket, but somehow everybody now seems much better informed." The excitement that day was about a media theme day coming up for eighth graders that would let them dress up (or down) to look like their favorite character.

Tommy Hilfiger, the Gap, and The Limited may have put the Y-ers on the best dressed list, but teachers have to get these students past basking in their trappings to think critically about living in the world they will inherit. Why should this be difficult for confident, advantaged children who have been empowered by their parents to be everything they can be? They are not rebellious and pessimistic about life like the Gen-Xers. They have grown up in a multicultural society and are coming to understand the need to face up to the dilemmas associated with globalization. They grasp the problems caused by drugs and sexual promiscuity. They know more about environmental concerns than any previous generation. They deplore worldwide violence. But despite knowing all of this, they find it difficult to seriously pay attention to consequential, world-impacting issues because they have grown up with an individualized, internal focus. They slept in Baby Dior infant coveralls, spent Saturdays at children's museums, and vacationed at theme parks designed for America's youth. It isn't difficult to understand their sense of self-importance.

School is a difficult place for children to attract singular attention, however, because they are in constant competition with their peers in a variety of social and academic arenas. For some, spiked hair or body piercing brings more attention than acing a biology test. For some, scoring a winning goal brings the needed attention. For others, defying the teacher in a show of power garners attention. For still others, dressing in racy T-shirts that say SEXY or FLIRT across the chest and short shorts that say BOOTYLICIOUS across the bottom does the trick.

Students who feel undervalued or misunderstood in school claim boredom to attract attention. Students who experience a sense of disconnection between what goes on in the classroom and what goes on outside of the classroom cite educational irrelevance as a means of calling attention to their dilemma. Whatever ploy is used by Generation Y, lack of individual attention is the primary underlying reason for not liking school, not completing work, failing a class, or even dropping out of school.

The unparalleled crisis facing teachers is not how to further individualize instruction to dispel boredom or how to improve instructional strategies to increase individual achievement, but rather how to awaken each and every student to the necessity of collectively creating a culture that will meaningfully address society's future. Cooperative group work teaches teamwork and provides positive social support for teaching students how to construct knowledge to solve a problem. Nevertheless, cooperative learning is a process and not a fixative for teaching children to think critically. When children enter school concerned only about their own interests, then teachers must take responsibility for attending to what should be a red-flag alert.

The shortsightedness of urging students to actively study only what is interesting to them and to pursue what provides individual gratification has created a divisive, cancerous apathy in the classroom. Such instruction does offer students individual attention, but it reinforces the importance of the individual to the detriment of the purpose for learning. Additionally, it undermines the significance of critical discernment and analytical thought that helps students to understand alternative points of view. In this era of accountability and measurability, teachers need to take a daring stance regarding what students should learn and how that learning should occur. What matters when students leave school is that they are able to understand how to live and work together in an emerging world that scarcely recognizes the individual.

This means teachers must educate students for more than subject-area content, for more than what's practical in the workplace, and for more than what interests individual students for personal gain. This means that teachers must urge students to "look at things as if they could be otherwise."[10] Teaching students to dissect issues is far more difficult than teaching them to dissect frogs. Teaching them to delve into the world of ideas is fraught with danger. Leading them across borders and into new intellectual territory is dangerous teaching. It also eschews measurement. I believe this is the only way children will learn to live with their inheritance and safeguard it for those who follow them. Teaching students to think deeply, critically, and analytically is our best chance for educational reform and the best hope for the rising millennials to get the attention they seek.

NOTES

1. Charles Derber, *The Pursuit of Attention: Power and Ego in Everyday Life* (New York: Oxford University Press, 2000), 34–37.

2. "The Celebrity 100," *Forbes.com,* 2002, at www.forbes.com/static_html/celebs/2002.html (accessed June 28, 2002).

3. "The Celebrity 100," *Forbes.com.*

4. The term *stage mother* refers to the parent who spends an exorbitant amount of time, effort, and money pursuing public fame and fortune for her or his child. Such parents traditionally act as sponsors, coaches, mentors, and the like, "off stage" while thrusting their child into the limelight.

5. Patrick Bellamy, "Main Event: The Murder of JonBenet Ramsey," *The Crime Library,* 1996, at www.crimelibrary.com/ramsey main.htm (accessed June 23, 2002).

6. Bob Bigelow, "Is Your Child Too Young for Youth Sports or Is Your Adult Too Old?" in *Sports in School,* ed. John R. Gerdy (New York: Teachers College Press, 2000), 7.

7. "Hockey Dad Death Trial Starts Today," *The Boston Channel.com,* 2002, at www.thebostonchannel.com/News/1160342/ (accessed June 25, 2002).

8. *Cooperative learning* refers to a collaborative learning strategy for students that combines the concept of combining positive interdependence with personal accountability for learning. It was first identified by researchers David W. Johnson and Roger T. Johnson, directors of the Cooperative Learning Center, at the University of Minnesota. For additional information about the Cooperative Learning Center and a list of publications by the authors access http://www.clcrc.com. The 7th edition of *Cooperation in the Classroom,* David W. Johnson, Roger T. Johnson, and Edythe J. Holubec (1998), Burgess Publishing Co., is also a helpful resource.

9. "Introducing Gen Y" and "Media Usage Trends," *Faces of the New Millennium,* at pubweb.nwu.edu/~eyc345/finalmedia.html, 1999 (accessed June 20, 2002).

10. Maxine Greene, *The Dialectic of Freedom* (New York: Teachers College Press, 1988), 55.

Epilogue: Popular Culture and Pedagogy

Fashion is not something that exists in dresses only. Fashion is in the sky, in the street, fashion has to do with ideas, the way we live, what is happening.

—Coco Chanel

People have immersed themselves in the moment for as long as time has existed. The moment is precisely what drives the entire popular culture industry. By the time a concept, trend, or product becomes "popular," a new development is already erupting. The International Best Dressed List offers an example of this phenomenon. Eleanor Lambert, "the grand dame of fashion publicity,"[1] first created the International Best Dressed List sixty-two years ago from a world-wide fashion poll she initiated. Each spring Lambert leaks the announcement of the names of those selected for the "List" to the press at a luncheon called expressly for that purpose. She defends the "List" and her role as organizer of the concept in this way: "This poll, conducted annually since 1940 with the help of an international committee of fashion authorities, has as its sole purpose the maintenance of a continuous historical record of fashion evolution, marked by a list of prominent personalities who, in the opinion [of] voters and their finalizing committee, has significantly personified that year's most memorable expression of influential personal style."[2] What she doesn't comment on is the "List's" overt promotion of the careers of fashion designers—"virtually everyone who has mattered in fashion, from Mollie Parnis and Anne Klein to Norman Norell and Bill Blass."[3]

Eleanor Lambert, a public relations mogul and the senior member of the fashion industry at ninety-eight years old, created the Best Dressed List to give the fashion industry an economic boost at the outbreak of World War II. In the "List's" earliest days, those who made it on the roster were primarily wealthy society women who were able to spend excessive amounts of money on their seasonal wardrobes. For twenty-five years, the Best Dressed List set the pace for fashion—haute couture for the privileged few and designer knockoffs for the average consumer. When Jackie Kennedy, fashion-conscious first lady, donned pillbox hats and knee-length shift dresses, women across the country tried to emulate the Jackie look. Although the cultural revolutions of the 1960s ended the era of fashion dictatorship, the list continues as a cultural symbol of our society, a "barometer not only of costume but of politics and culture."[4]

I doubt that many people could name anyone on the 2001–2002 Best Dressed List, but the fashion industry itself remains a viable example of the strength of contemporary pop culture. Clothing styles identify epochs in history and continue to make a statement about the changing political and cultural landscape of the times. A patriotic trend hit the marketplace following September 11, 2001, for example, with variations of stars and stripes emblazoned on everything from baseball caps to BVDs. Back-to-school fashions annually lure millions of school-age consumers, or their parents, into purchasing clothes of the moment. One year, the rapster look is the rage, and the next year, the peasant look takes the stage. Regardless of the fashion, wearing up-to-date clothing makes students feel like valued members of their school community. The clothing itself spins a tale about the nation's social and political climate.

The language people use, the clothes they wear, the stories they tell, the goods they consume, and the behavior they exhibit are all indicators of what constitutes worth in a community. An educational system that doesn't consciously include aspects of the culture that people value will not meet the needs of the society it serves.

The public expects good teachers to move students from *A* to *Z* as they facilitate their learning and encourage them to stretch beyond themselves in learning how to learn. To the uninitiated, this might seem like a simple task easily measured by end-of-year tests. To the experienced teacher, this is a career feat. Standardized tests won't measure why tenth-grade students can discuss the characters, plot, and theme of a favorite movie with mature insight and eloquent detail but can't pick out the same elements from a short story. Nor will the tests account for why students are readily able to explain the meaning of dense rap lyrics but find it difficult to understand a simple maxim like "A bird in the hand is worth two in the bush." Teachers know only too well that teaching to benchmark tests has little to do with teacher accountability and even less to do with educating students for life in a democratic society. They need to bravely shift the focus from the textbook to society and to thoughtfully question how they can best challenge students to learn.

Each semester, I ask students who are completing the last few months of their teacher preparation program to comment in writing about their fears and hopes for teaching as viewed from their limited experience. Invariably, prospective teachers indicate concerns about the unexpected amount of time that they spend on preparing good lessons, about the amount of time that classroom discipline takes away from teaching, and about the preponderance of paperwork called for by school districts. They look forward to having the freedom to teach in their own classrooms and to providing a positive and hopeful environment for learning. Similar comments from new teachers haven't substantially changed in a decade, but society has. The classroom teacher needs to attend in new ways to what the reality of providing a hopeful environment for teaching signifies.

Today's teacher must seek a pedagogy that captures contemporary issues in a culturally relevant context and then use that pedagogy to move students beyond the insubstantial moment. This doesn't call for teachers to entirely abandon classical methods for teaching or to ignore meaningful content in the liberal arts and sciences or to ignore skills needed for the workplace. It does call for teachers to use popular culture as a pedagogical tool. Teachers need to be alert to the message their pedagogy sends to students and to society. What message does teaching with an imageless methodology communicate when today's children live in an image-driven world? What message does a classroom overflowing with manufactured manipulatives communicate about consumer responsibility?

Teachers who understand how culture shapes behavior and gives meaning to student behavior, interaction, and interest in learning will see the convergence of culture, popular culture, and the classroom as a positive dynamic. These teachers will give critical attention to deciphering the educational needs of their students in a context that is culturally relevant to their students. They will seek textual and cultural substance in the content they teach. They will risk crossing borders and setting boundaries in exercising the freedom to teach. They will dare to take time for reflection in a fast-forward world and provide time for their students to learn to do the same.

Teachers must reclaim the classroom, not for themselves, not from society, but for society. They need to end the us-versus-them contest that has marred the profession and work in relationship with society and its ever-evolving culture. They must question limited descriptions of educational reality, revise the frameworks that have bound teachers for centuries, and imagine the classroom as something quite different from what it has been for too long.

NOTES

1. Catherine Fitzpatrick, "Sorting Out Fashion Week Sideshows," *Milwaukee Journal Sentinel Online,* 2002, at www.jsonline.com//lifestyle/fashion/feb02/19482. asp (accessed June 1, 2002).

2. Ernest Schmatolla, "The Daily NY Fashion Blog, 2002," at www. lookonline.com/2002_02_01_archive.html (accessed June 1, 2002).

3. Jack O'Dwyer, "O'Dwyer's PR Daily, 2000," at www.odwyerpr.com/jack_ odwyers_nl2000/0503.htm (accessed June 1, 2002).

4. David Patrick Columbia, "Best-Dressed List Recalls a Lost Age and Connects and Reflects the New," *New York Social Diary.com,* 2002, at www. newyorksocialdiary.com/archive/socialdiary4.2.02.html (accessed June 1, 2002).

About the Author

Dr. Susan Huber is an associate professor in the educational leadership department of the School of Education at the University of St. Thomas, St. Paul/Minneapolis, Minnesota. Although she considers herself first and foremost a teacher, she has served in a number of administrative capacities during her sixteen years in academe, including dean, associate dean, and department chair. Prior to her career in higher education, she was principal of a P–8 school and taught both English and Latin at the secondary level. She has worked extensively with teachers and principals in public and private schools as an educator and consultant and serves on many educational committees, task forces, and boards.

Huber finds studying the daily rituals of people and their interactions with one another fascinating work. Schools provide especially rich research venues because they depict society in microcosmic form. She teaches education foundation courses and qualitative research and is particularly interested in symbolic interaction.

She is married and the mother of two sons.